GREAT
FAMILY
DAYS OUT

**POCKET
GOOD
GUIDES**

GOOD GUIDES

POCKET GOOD GUIDES

GREAT FAMILY DAYS OUT

EDITED BY ALISDAIR AIRD

DEPUTY EDITOR FIONA STAPLEY

ASSOCIATE EDITORS: KAREN FICK, ROBERT UNSWORTH

RESEARCH OFFICER: ELIZABETH ADLINGTON

ADDITIONAL RESEARCH: CATHERINE SHEPPERD

EBURY PRESS

First published in Great Britain in 2002
Ebury Press
Random House
20 Vauxhall Bridge Road
London SW1 2SA.

10 9 8 7 6 5 4 3 2 1

Random House Australia (Pty) Limited
20 Alfred Street, Milsons Point
Sydney
New South Wales 2061, Australia

Random House New Zealand Limited
18 Poland Road, Glenfield, Auckland 10
New Zealand

Random House South Africa (Pty) Limited
Endulini, 5A Jubilee Road
Parktown 2193
South Africa

Random House UK Limited Reg. No. 954009

www.randomhouse.co.uk

A CIP catalogue record for this book is available from the British Library

ISBN 0091885175

Papers used by Ebury Press are natural, recyclable products made from wood grown in sustainable forests

Typeset by Textype, Cambridge
Cover design by Nim Design
Front cover image © ImageBank
Printed and bound in Denmark by Nørhaven Paperback A/S, Viborg

Introduction

The best of Britain – by the day

The Good Guides team, whose top-selling list of successes includes the annual *Good Britain Guide*, has now turned its eagle eyes on family days out. From the vast range of possibilities, the team have short-listed over 200 outings. Although the main holiday areas are particularly well covered, the team has searched out rewarding places to visit and things to do throughout Great Britain, whether in big cities or in quiet countryside.

Besides the best theme parks and other traditional family attractions from zoos to castles and steam trains to boat trips, this book includes plenty of unexpected delights. Some of the outings are places where you could happily spend most of a day. Others link together two or more different places, to fill a day – although of course you could decide to go to just one of them. For all the outings, the team has concentrated on real family enjoyment, searching its database of up-to-date information on many thousands of places to visit to pick out the top days out.

The Good Guides team also has unrivalled expertise in the field of informal eating out. Backed by over 45,000 recent confidential reports from readers and its own anonymous inspections, its recommendations for nearby family meals add an extra dimension of pleasure to many of these outings.

To contact the Pocket Good Guides team, please write to

Great Family Days Out
Freepost TN1 569
Wadhurst
E. Sussex
TN5 7BR

or check out
www.goodguides.co.uk

Contents

Using this book ix

South-East England & The Midlands 1

Leicestershire & Rutland 2

Warwickshire 4

Northamptonshire 10

Cambridgeshire 12

Norfolk 16

Suffolk 18

Essex 22

Hertfordshire 28

Bedfordshire 30

Buckinghamshire 34

Oxfordshire 36

Berkshire 40

Wiltshire 44

Isle of Wight 48

Hampshire 50

Surrey 60

Sussex 62

Kent 66

London 72

South-West England & Southern Wales 81

Dyfed 82
Mid Glamorgan 84
Gwent 84
S Glamorgan 86
Shropshire 88
Herefordshire 90
Gloucs 96
Worcestershire 92
Somerset 100
Dorset 108
Devon 112
Cornwall 118

Northern England & North Wales 127

Cumbria 128
Northumbria 132
Lancashire 136
Yorkshire 144
Lincolnshire 156
Nottinghamshire 160
Derbyshire 164
Staffordshire 168
Cheshire 172
Shropshire 176
Clwyd 178
Gwynedd 180
Powys 184

Scotland 187

South 188
East 196
West 200
North 200

Maps 202

Using this book

The regions and the maps

We have split Great Britain into four regions (see Contents). Each region has a double-page map at the end of the book. Within each region, our recommended outings are numbered. These numbers are shown on the map for each region. The place names shown on the map are just to give you an idea of which cities the various outings are closest to.

Special events

Often, you can build a great day out around some special event. Our web site, www.goodguides.co.uk, includes an easily searched calendar of several thousand special events, country-wide. All you need to do is pick a day, and you can see what's happening where. The web site also includes some detailed recommended day-out tours in the Lake District and Brighton, as extras to this book.

It's also worth knowing about European Heritage Open Days. On these, many notable buildings will be open to the public which are normally closed. English National Heritage Weekend will be on 14–15 September, over 2,000 properties will be open. As we went to press individual details are undecided, but if 2001 was anything to go by they will range from intriguing follies through all sorts of official and office buildings to even the Chancellor of the Exchequer's office. For more information ring (020) 7930 0914 or look at their web site: www.civictrust.org.uk. The Welsh Civic Trust run open weekends through most of September, ring (029) 20 484606 for details. The Scottish equivalent, Doors Open Days, takes in over 700 properties and will run most weekends in September; ring (0141) 221 1466. During London Open House

Weekend, 21–22 September, there will be free admission to around 100 buildings; anything from Lloyds of London to Bushy House. For more details write to London Open House, PO Box 6984, London, N6 6PY or call (020) 7267 2070.

Prices and other factual details

Information about opening times and so forth is for 2002. In a very few cases establishments were uncertain about these when the *Guide* went to press; if so, we say in the text. (And of course there's always the risk of changed plans and unexpected closures.) When we say 'cl Nov–Mar' we mean closed from the beginning of November to the end of March, inclusive; however when we say 'cl Nov–Easter' we mean that the establishment reopens for Easter.

Where establishments were able to guarantee a price for 2002, we have marked this with an asterisk. In many cases establishments could not rule out an unscheduled price increase, and in these cases – ie, no asterisk against the price – it's probably prudent to allow for a small increase by the summer of 2002.

The heritage organisations

NT after price details means that the property is owned by the National Trust, and that for members of the Trust admission is free. There is a similar arrangement for properties owned by the National Trust for Scotland (NTS); the two Trusts have a reciprocal arrangement, so that members of one may visit the properties of the other free. Membership is therefore well worth while if you are likely to visit more than a very few properties in the year – quite apart from its benefit to the Trusts' valuable work. NT membership is £31 a year (£58 family membership); details from National Trust, PO Box 39, Bromley, Kent BR1 3XL, (0208) 315 1111. NTS membership is £28 (£47 family); details from National Trust for Scotland, 28 Charlotte Sq, Edinburgh EH2 4ET, (0131) 243 9300.

EH stands for English Heritage, HS for Historic Scotland, and Cadw for the organisation in charge of Welsh historic buildings. All three organisations have a similar membership scheme, giving free entry to those of their properties which charge for admission.

Disabled access

We always ask establishments if they can deal well with disabled people. We mention disabled access if a cautious view of their answers suggests that this is reasonable, though to be on the safe side anyone with a serious mobility problem would be well advised to ask ahead (many establishments tell us that this helps them to make any special arrangements needed). There may well be at least some access even when we or the establishment concerned have not felt it safe to make a blanket recommendation – again, well worth checking ahead. There are of course many places where we can't easily make this sort of assessment – particularly the less formal 'attractions' such as bird reserves, waterside walks, viewpoints. In such cases (which should be obvious from the context) the absence of any statement about disabled access doesn't mean that a visit is out of the question, it simply means we have no information about that aspect. We're always grateful to hear of readers' own experiences. An important incidental point: many places told us that they would give free admission to a wheelchair user and companion.

South-East England & The Midlands

Including Bedfordshire, Berkshire, Buckinghamshire, Cambridgeshire, Essex, Hampshire, Hertfordshire, Isle of Wight, Kent, Leicestershire, London, Norfolk, Northamptonshire, Oxfordshire, Rutland, Suffolk, Surrey, Sussex, Warwickshire, Wiltshire and the West Midlands, and London.

SEE MAP I

1. Shrink yourself on the forest floor

Conkers (B5003 W of Ashby-de-la-Zouch) Really enjoyable for a family day out, with lots of computer interactives and hands-on exhibits – you can try on bats' ears, climb inside a leaf, smell a rotting mouse and be squirted by a gigantic wood ant at the new visitor centre Conkers Discovery; a train ride will take you the ¼ mile between here and the former Heart of the Forest National Visitor Centre – now Conkers Waterside. 120 acres of new walks and landscaped trails through traditional broadleaf woodland have been recently opened; there are picnic places, lakes, an assault course, sculpture trail, canopy walk, and not just an adventure playground but even an activity trail for adults.

Moira Furnace and Craft Workshops Along the same road as Conkers, this recently restored 19th-c blast furnace has interactive displays about the operation of the furnace, a few craft workshops, woodland walks and a children's play area. Meals, snacks, shop, disabled access; cl Mon, plus Tues in winter, 25–26 Dec and 1 Jan; (01283) 224667; £3 inc 30-min boat trip on the canal.

2. Snibston Discovery Park

(Ashby Rd, Coalville) Busy 100-acre site, based around a former colliery (the first shaft was sunk by George and Robert Stephenson). Its exhibitions and displays cover a varied range of topics connected to science and industry. Each section has hands-on or working exhibits; children like the Science Alive gallery best, with plenty of experiments and activities – there's even the illusion of cycling with a skeleton. Similarly organised galleries look at transport, mining and fashion. For an extra charge (50p), there's an incredible virtual reality experience: you find yourselves in the middle of an exploding oil rig and have to make a dash for the helicopter pad. The landscaped grounds include a huge play area, nature reserve, sculpture trail, and picnic areas, with extra charges for fishing, and the evocative tours of the mine workings by former pitmen. Meals, snacks, shop, disabled access; cl 25–26 Dec and a week in Jan; (01530) 278444; £4.75.

3. Apes in all shapes

Twycross Zoo Park (A444, Twycross) Specialises in primates, with an enormous range of apes, gibbons, orang-utans, and chimpanzees – every shape, size and species. Plenty of other animals too, inc giraffes, sealions, elephants and penguins; the reptile house is 20p extra. Can get crowded on summer afternoons. Meals, snacks, shop, disabled access; cl 25 Dec; (01827) 880250; £6.50.

You could combine a visit here with a trip on the **Battlefield Steam Railway Line**, which runs from Shackerstone through

Market Bosworth to Shenton by Bosworth Battlefield, a rather nice return trip of just over nine miles. There's a Victorian tearoom at the Shackerstone end (open only if trains running), and some displays. Trains usually run wknds and bank hols Mar–Oct, plus Weds pm Jul–Aug; (01827) 880754 for timetable; £5 return. The friendly Hercules in nearby Sutton Cheney has a good choice of bar lunches (and the landlord was a Wolves footballer).

The railway gets its name from the Battle of Bosworth Field, which won the English crown for the Tudors. A visitor centre has explanatory films and exhibitions, as well as a detailed trail following the sites of the fighting. Snacks, shop, disabled access; cl am, Mon–Fri in Mar, plus Sat Nov–Dec, and all Jan–Feb (01455) 290429; £3 entry plus £1 for parking.

4. National Space Science Centre

(Exploration Drive, off Corporation Rd, Leicester) Anyone who's ever looked up at the sky and wondered will be enthralled by this excellent new centre, which opened not long before we went to press. Everything in space, from stars and planets to rockets and satellites, is presented, in an accessible and informative way, using the latest technology and hundreds of interactive and hands-on displays. It cost £52 million, and it shows – particularly in the extraordinary 41-metre (135-ft) tower visible for miles around, created not to be ostentatious, but to house their biggest rockets, Blue Streak and Thor Able. There are good views of the city from the top, and the glass lifts give a dramatic look at the rockets as you float up past them. At the heart of the place is an outstanding planetarium, with much better shows than you'll have seen anywhere else; they currently have a film exploring the sheer size of the universe, and one specially for under-5s. You'll get a timed ticket when you go into the main centre. The first of the four main galleries, Into Space, looks at what it takes to be an astronaut, answering those intriguing questions such as how you eat or go to the loo in space. Exploring the Universe concentrates on how everything began, and whether there's anyone out there; The Planets colourfully examines our own solar system; and Orbiting Earth looks at how space technology affects our everyday lives. Along the way you can feel what it's like to be blasted into space, launch your own rocket, design your own alien, see pieces of the moon or Mars, and try your hand at forecasting the weather. A final section looks at the latest space happenings (any launches can be shown live), with staff to answer questions. Fascinating but fun too, it takes around three hours to see everything, though if you're a real space nut you could end up staying longer. Meals and snacks (with rockets suspended above you), shop, good disabled access; cl Mon during term-time (and am Mon in the hols), also 25–26 Dec and 1 Jan; (0870) 607 7223; £7.50 adults, £5.50 children 5–14. A family ticket for two adults and two children is £22; two adults and three children is £27. You can buy tickets up to a month in advance by phone, at branches of Tower Records, or at some branches of Waitrose and HMV – though there is a booking fee.

5. Rutland Water

Europe's biggest man-made lake, oddly shaped, with a number of attractions. On the N side of the lake are nature trails, an unusual drought garden created by the late Geoff Hamilton, places to hire bikes, and hourly BOAT TRIPS; (01572) 787630. You can fish in various parts of the water with a centre down at Normanton, which also has a small MUSEUM in a church modelled on London's St John's, Smith Sq. The refreshingly informal Normanton Park Hotel here has good food, as does the White Horse at Empingham, and there are plenty of good places for picnics.

Butterfly & Aquatic Centre (off A606 Empingham–Whitwell) Next to the main Rutland Water information centre, there's a butterfly house with a good water feature, and various other insects and reptiles; also a video on the reservoir's construction in the 1970s. Snacks, shop, disabled access; cl Nov–Mar; (01780) 460515; £3.50.

Lyndon Bird Reserve (off Lyndon–Manton rd) Well set up for the non-specialist, this has a useful visitor centre, occasional summer crafts, and a variety of walks, talks and events. Disabled access; reserve usually open all year, visitor centre open all wknds, plus Tues–Thurs May–Oct; (01572) 737378; £2. The **Egleton Reserve** (Uppingham Rd) is aimed at the more serious bird-watcher, with a comfortable purpose-built observation centre. Varied talks, walks and events; (01572) 770651; snacks, shop, excellent disabled access; cl 25–26 Dec; £4.

6. Waterside fun from bottle-fed animals to jet bikes

Kingsbury Water Park (Bodymoor Heath) 30 lakes and pools, created by gravel excavations, in 600 landscaped acres. Waterside and woodland walks, nature trails (maps and leaflets at the visitor centre), and two play areas. You can fish (from £1.80, under-16s fish for free at Mitchell's Pool), and there's jet bike hire. Snacks, shop, disabled access; cl 25 Dec; (01827) 872660; free, £2.20 for parking. The park also contains **Broomey Croft Children's Farm**; all the usual farm animals for children to feed, plus tractor rides, activities from bottle-feeding lambs to shoeing horses, and a play area (with a bit set aside for the under-4s). Snacks, shop, disabled access; usually open daily Apr–Sept and Oct half-term, plus wknds Oct–Mar, cl 25–26 Dec; (01827) 873844; £2.80. The canalside Dog & Doublet has decent food.

7. Cadbury World

(Linden Rd, Bournville, Birmingham) Anyone who's ever tucked into a Cadbury's product will find something to interest them at this jolly place – not a factory tour, but a specially built centre next door, with all you could feasibly want to know about how their chocolates are made and marketed. Displays can throw up alarming statistics: for example, if you set out to eat Cadbury's annual output at the rate of one bar every five minutes, it would take you 16,000 years. The history of chocolate is given something of a corporate bias (you could be forgiven for thinking nobody has ever made it apart from the Aztecs and the Cadburys), and no one's pretending they're not just trying to flog more of their goodies, but the exhibitions have been put together with a real sense of fun. Children in particular get a lot out of it; many of the major parts have been specially designed with younger visitors in mind, and there are plenty of buttons to press on the way round. Highlights for them include the interactive Cadbury Land show (a colourful film presented in a multi-sensory theatre), an alternative view of chocolate-making offered by Mr Cadbury's Parrot in the Fantasy Factory, and Cadabra – a nicely silly ride through an imaginative themed world in a car shaped like a cocoa bean. But what really sticks in the memory (and around the mouth) is the chance to sample fresh liquid chocolate, straight from the vat; you can have a go at dipping it into moulds. Older visitors may prefer the nostalgic Cadbury's TV adverts from the last 40 years (some from overseas), and there's a collection of period wrappers shown in a 1930s-style sweet shop. Depending when you visit, you may see a genuine packaging plant, with Fruit & Nut bars being wrapped. There's also an exhibition on how they make the chocolate ads that start and finish *Coronation Street*. The outdoor play area is good – and useful for burning off chocolate-caused calories; there are plenty of picnic tables next to it. A typical visit lasts a little over two hours (most of it under cover), but you'll need to book in advance to be sure of getting in; on popular days, tickets can be sold out well in advance, and if you just turn up you may find they're full. Meals, snacks, good shop (some bargains and unique varieties), mostly disabled access; open daily Mar–Oct, and usually wknds and at least a couple of other days Nov–Feb – best to check then, though you may sometimes have to wait to get through; (0121) 451 4180; £8.25 adults, £6.25 children 4–15; a family ticket for two adults and two children is £25, two adults and three children £30.

For a complete contrast, the **Birmingham Nature Centre** (Pershore Rd) is refreshing: British and European animals in indoor and outdoor enclosures designed to resemble natural habitats. Meals and snacks, shop, disabled access; cl Sun Nov–Feb; (0121) 472 7775; £1.50.

8. Thinktank

(Millennium Point Centre, Curzon St, Birmingham) This impressive £50m new science centre, the Midlands' biggest, has ten galleries on four floors. There's a huge amount for children of all ages here; each gallery has a different theme, and some are aimed at specific ages (Kids in the City has lots of fun for the under-7s, while the medical gallery Things About Me is aimed at children under 11). The emphasis is on getting involved, and there are more than 200 interactive exhibits – you can take the controls of a digger, carry out a virtual hip operation, or track down a jewel thief, and there are various activity trails and games. Large exhibits include a steam locomotive and the world's oldest working steam engine, Spitfire and Hurricane aircraft, and a racing car. Temporary exhibitions, and lots of special events wknds and school hols. As well as all that, there's the region's first IMAX cinema here too. Meals, snacks, shop, disabled access; cl Fri; (0121) 464 1977; £6.50, £6 for the IMAX.

9. National Sea Life Centre

(Waters Edge, Brindley Pl Birmingham) The flagship of the excellent Sea Life Centre chain that we recommend in quite a few resorts around the country. The hi-tech displays are both fun and instructive, with around 3,000 native British marine and freshwater creatures shown off in careful re-creations of their natural habitats, also themed soft play area and a reconstructed *Titanic* wreck. The highlight is a walk-through tube designed to give the impression of walking above the sea bed, with sharks, rays and other creatures swimming above, alongside and beneath you. Norman Foster designed the building. Meals, snacks, shop, disabled access; cl 25 Dec; (0121) 633 4700; *£8.

Reputedly there are more canals in Birmingham than in Venice, and the redevelopment of old canal buildings has brought a lively new focus of restaurants, bars, hotels and offices to this whole Gas St/Brindley Pl area, with plenty of crafts and entertainments too.

10. Black Country Living Museum

(Tipton Rd, 1m N of Dudley centre) Good value well thought out open-air museum (with much under cover) giving a good feel of how things used to be in the Black Country, the heavily industrialised and proudly individual areas in the W part of the Birmingham conurbation. It's an authentically reconstructed turn-of-the-century village, complete with cottages, chapel, chemist, baker, pub, and trips into limestone caverns (summer only) or even down a mine, as well as black and white comedies from Laurel and

Hardy or Harold Lloyd in the old cinema, school lessons in the school room, and an old-fashioned working fairground just outside the village (Mar–Nov; extra charges for some rides). Staff in period costumes illustrate traditional crafts and test-drive old vehicles, and there are plenty of extra activities for children during school holidays. Meals and snacks (and space for picnics), shop, mostly disabled access (it may be worth calling first); cl Mon and Tues Nov–Feb, and several days over Christmas, best to phone; (0121) 557 9643; £7.95.

11. Warwick Castle

(Castle Hill, Warwick) One of the country's most splendid castles, this is a lively place, with plenty for children to enjoy (especially in summer). Several displays showing the influence of the Tussauds group, who own the site, but purists shouldn't be put off by the gloss or waxwork figures; the rooms are excellently preserved, and their fine furnishings and art well worth braving the crowds for. The marvellous grounds were designed by Capability Brown, and as well as the delightful gardens, have pleasant strolls along the banks of the River Avon; the views from the parklands are dramatic. Meals, snacks, shop, disabled access to grounds only; cl 25 Dec; (0870) 4422000; £11.50, £10.25 in winter.

St John's House (St John's, Warwick) 17th-c house with exhibits from the county museum, a changing collection of costumes, several room reconstructions, and an under-5s discovery room. Shop, disabled access to ground floor only; cl all Mons (exc bank hols), plus Sun end Sept–Apr; (01926) 412132; free.

The Saxon Mill (Guy's Cliffe) is a prettily placed waterside family dining pub on the edge of Warwick.

12. Hundreds of historic cars, and the estate where Shakespeare went poaching

Heritage Motor Centre (Banbury Rd, Gaydon) Busy centre with the world's biggest collection of historic British cars – 300 in all, starting with an 1895 Wolseley. Also hundreds of drawings, photographs, trophies and models, hi-tech displays and video shows. There's a 4-wheel-drive demo circuit, quad bike track, and a nature reserve. The design of the building is incredible, esp inside. Meals, snacks, shop, disabled access; cl 24–26 Dec; (01926) 641188; £8. The Malt Shovel has good value food.

    Charlecote Park (Charlecote) 250 acres of parkland, full of deer (Shakespeare is said to have poached here), along with the descendants of reputedly the country's first flock of Jacob sheep. Well furnished Great Hall and Victorian kitchen, an impressive Tudor gatehouse, and a garden designed by Sir Edmund Fairfax Lucy. Playground, meals, snacks, shop, disabled access; open Fri–Tues Apr–Oct (cl Good Fri), wknds Nov–Mar; (01789) 470277; £5.60; NT. By the park is a charming little 19th-c estate village of timbered cottages, and a show Victorian church. In nearby pretty Hampton Lucy, which has a lovely church, the Boars Head has decent food.

13. Britain's first theme park?

Wicksteed Park (off A6, S outskirts of Kettering) Big amusement park set up in 1921 when they introduced boating on the lake. Some older features still remain (an antique roundabout for example), and more modern attractions include a monorail, roller-coaster and films in the Cine 2000 dome. It's still relatively low-key compared to other leisure parks – thrill rides here are mainly of the Dodgems, ferris wheel and pirate ship type – but for many visitors that's precisely the appeal. A children's playground has been added recently, and further rides are planned for summer 2002. The grounds are very pleasant for a stroll, with a pitch and putt course, various well laid out gardens, an aviary, paddling pools, and free play areas for younger children. New bistro, shop, disabled access, open May–Sept; (01536) 512475; £5 parking charge (less out of season, or after 3pm), then you buy vouchers for the rides, or a wristband with a day's unlimited rides for £7.50, £11.50 for children.

14. Falcons fly at England's once-largest house

Holdenby House, Gardens & Falconry Centre (Holdenby) This fine-looking house was originally eight times the size it is now, and the largest house in Elizabethan England. It was a Royal palace for part of the 17th c, and subsequently a prison, holding the captured King Charles I at the end of the Civil War. In the afternoon on Easter, spring and summer bank hol Mons, you can look around the house with its collection of rare and unusual pianos, and there are very good special events and extra activities for children. They've a splendid collection of birds of prey, with regular flying displays of buzzards, owls and kestrels. The 20-acre gardens are lovely, with an Elizabethan-style garden laid out by Rosemary Verey that includes only plants that would have been grown in 1580. The family who live here (the Lowthers) have had more MPs than any other clan. Teas, shop, limited disabled access; open Sun pm and bank hols Easter–end Sept, and pm daily exc Sat July and Aug. On event days admission is £5, other times £3.

The Brampton Halt (Pitsford Rd, off A5199) over at Chapel Brampton has decent food. Beside it, the enthusiastic **Northampton & Lamport Railway** has short train rides and special events throughout the summer – ring to check times

(01604) 820327. Snacks, shop, disabled access to train (but not to facilities); £3. Its name is a proud commitment to growth northwards, but for the time being the 14-mile walk and cycle way through pretty countryside by the line is a very pleasant foretaste.

15. The past comes alive at Sulgrave Manor

(Sulgrave, off B4525) The ancestral home of George Washington's family, this modest manor is exceptional for families during their regular special events, when the whole place returns to how it would have been during a particular period. They seem less concerned with making money than with trying to spark real interest in the past in children – and of course the most direct way of doing that is to bring it to life around them. People in period costume go about their daily business, and children can take part in a wide range of activities from wassailing or helping in the kitchen at Christmas, to joining in the harvest during their Apple Day Festival. Very well done, and sincere without being overly earnest, these events are so popular with some visitors that they'll come back several times each year. Their annual Tudor Christmas (wknds in December) is always fun and particularly atmospheric; other events over the next year include a weekend of Tudor Easter customs, a Food Festival with samples of traditional English food through the ages (27–28 Apr), a Local History week between 4 and 12 May that will involve the whole village (and include a May Day Festival on the Monday), a big re-creation of life in Stuart times (1–4 Jun), a Needlework Festival (3–8 Aug), a Viking Living History weekend (24–26 Aug), their extensive Tudor Living History week (5–13 Oct), and the Apple Day Festival (19–20 Oct). The house is still worth a visit on non-event days, when they do guided tours, though it's mainly adults (and school groups, who get to spend the day dressed as Tudors) who get the most out of it then. As well as elegant rooms and well kept gardens, there are several relics of Washington, though he never lived here – it was his great-great-grandfather who emigrated to America. They have an outdoor theatre in late July. Snacks, shop, some disabled access; open for events as above, plus house open pm Apr–Oct, cl Mon and Fri (exc bank hols or during events), and for prebooked groups open any time exc Jan; (01295) 760205; around £6 on event days, otherwise £5 adults (£2.50 children 5–16). On fine days, children can have lunch in the garden of the Star, an attractive pub just down the road (they're not allowed inside).

16. Waterfowl and water sports

Waterfowl World (Peakirk) Over 100 different species of waterfowl inc rare and unusual breeds, all in a lovely setting. Most were reared in captivity and can be fed by hand – always fun; they sell corn in the gatehouse but the birds seem to prefer bread, so take some along. A good outing even if you're not exactly a twitcher, fascinating if you are. Snacks, shop, disabled access; last entry 2pm Nov–Easter, cl 24–25 Dec; (01733) 252271; £3.50. The nearby Ruddy Duck is popular for lunch.

    Ferry Meadows Country Park (off A605 W of Peterborough) Useful for children to let off steam; 500 acres with play areas, two big lakes with water sports, fishing and boat trips, bird reserve, pony rides, miniature railway, and two golf courses and pitch and putt nearby. Visitor centre; snacks, shop, disabled access; (01733) 234443; free. Parking charge wknds and bank hols Apr–Oct, £2.40.

17. Haven for endangered species

Hamerton Zoo Park (Hamerton) A real favourite with some readers, this dedicated centre has a splendidly varied collection of rare and endangered species from all over the world. In over 15 acres of pretty countryside, there are over a hundred different species, from playful marmosets, lemurs and gibbons, through cheetahs, wolves and boa constrictors, to smaller animals such as tortoises and porcupines; they also have plenty of birds, and have recently acquired bengal and white tigers. Talks from the keepers at feeding times at wknds and school holidays. Covered walkways mean you can move between most of the animal houses without getting wet. Tearoom (cl in winter), small shop, disabled access; cl 25 Dec; (01832) 293362; £5.50. Their website, www.hamertonzoopark.com, usually has money-saving offers.

18. A great estate with lots to do

Wimpole Hall and Home Farm (Wimpole, off A603) The varied attractions at this huge estate can easily fill most of a day. Children like the working stock farm best, its thatched and timbered buildings designed by Sir John Soane when it was at the forefront of agricultural innovation. A restored barn houses machinery and tools from those days, and there are plenty of farm animals (with younger ones to pet and feed) inc various rare breeds; separate play areas for older and younger children. The mainly 18th-c house is one of the most striking mansions in the whole of East Anglia. Behind its imposing and harmonious Georgian façade is a lovely trompe l'oeil chapel ceiling, and rooms by James Gibbs and Sir John Soane. Perfect for a relaxing stroll, the gardens are good for spring daffodils; vegetables now grow in the restored walled garden. Best of all perhaps are the 360 acres of parkland, home to the National Walnut Collection, and designed by several different notable landscapers inc Capability Brown and Repton; the remains of a medieval village are under the pasture. Good programme of concerts and events in the hall or grounds. Meals, snacks, shops, some disabled access (not to house). Hall open pm Tues–Thurs and wknds mid-Mar to late Oct, plus bank hol and Fri pm in Aug. Farm open same times plus mornings, wknds in winter, and Fri in July and Aug; (01223) 207257; *£9 hall, farm and garden (£6.20 hall, £4.90 farm, £2.50 gardens); NT. The surrounding park is open all year, with walkers welcomed free of charge to the extensive paths and tracks through its farmland and woodland, past a folly and up to a surprisingly elevated ridge path. The handsome Hardwicke Arms has decent food.

19. Europe's greatest aircraft collection

Imperial War Museum, Duxford (just off M11, junction 10) Impossible to miss from the motorway, this big former airbase is a good deal more rewarding for children than you might expect, with plenty to look at apart from old planes, and a good deal of effort put into making the displays and exhibits both relevant and evocative. Best of all, it's free for children, so while a visit can easily stretch out to a whole day, it shouldn't end up costing too much money. Unmissable for anyone interested in aviation, it's home to Europe's best collection of military and civil aircraft, 180 in all, from flimsy-looking bi-planes to state-of-the-art Gulf War jets. Children can clamber into the cockpits of some of them, or, just as dramatic, walk right underneath. They also have a huge collection of tanks and military vehicles, and a naval collection inc midget submarines and helicopters. New exhibitions are added all the time: last year they opened the well put together Normandy Experience, which aims to show what life was like for the infantrymen in Normandy; you enter by crossing over a landing craft to the sound of gunfire. Children can pick up helmets and gunpacks, and imagine what it must have been like trying to run while wearing them. The most obvious recent addition is the American Air Museum, a collection of US combat aircraft in a remarkable new building by Norman Foster. There's a lively new simulator ride for children (small charge), summer narrow-gauge railway and an adventure playground, but many younger visitors find the main displays just as compelling: the preserved hangars, control towers and operations rooms have something of the atmosphere they must have had when this was a working base. The site covers about a mile; a bus can take you between the different bits. Each year they have several dramatic air shows (extra charge), and some planes still fly on other days. A free bus runs every hour from and to Cambridge Station; it takes about 20 minutes. Meals and snacks (and plenty of space for picnics), shop, good disabled access; cl 24–26 Dec; (01223) 835000; £7.70 adults, children free. The Green Man close by at Thriplow is an interesting place for lunch (but no under-5s allowed, and it's cl Tues).

20. Seal spotting in Blakeney

Boats leave from Morston Quay slightly W of Blakeney on the A149 coast rd once or twice a day Mar–Oct (times depend on the tide), and on most winter wknds; when the tide allows you'll also find trips wending their way down the creek from the little harbour at Blakeney itself. Most last two hours, which takes in an hour or so exploring the NT-owned bird reserve at Blakeney Point. The highlight comes just before that, when the boat goes past the sandbanks at the end of the Point, where dozens of grey and common seals lie basking happily in the sun. Several different operators run boats, with the smaller ones owned by the Beans our favourites. Booking a few days in advance is recommended (esp in summer, when there are crowds of visitors waiting on the quay), on (01263) 740038. £5. Local information centres have full details of operators and times.

Crabbing is fun from Blakeney too, and surprisingly successful. Also a (free) collection of waterfowl down by the harbour, long breezy walks, unspoilt flint cottages, broad sky and sea vistas, maybe even a seal pup on the beach in spring. There's a good dyke walk to Cley-next-the-Sea, with the birds on the mudflats for company. Blakeney has a very good tea shop; besides the Blakeney Hotel, the Manor, White Horse and Kings Arms are all good. In summer it gets packed.

21. Norfolk Wildlife Park

(A1067, Great Witchingham) Enthusiastic and committed new owners have taken over this 40-acre site, and though they don't plan any drastic changes (save a slight change to the name), regular visitors can expect to see quite a few cosmetic improvements over the next few months. They're also keen to put more of a focus on breeding and conservation: already they've introduced breeding colonies of red squirrels, and as we went to press were planning to do the same with barbary apes. In attractive parkland, the centre has a good range of mostly British and European wildlife, and everything from wallabies, lynxes and otters to tortoises, iguanas and snakes. They've recently added a walk-through subtropical parakeet aviary, and birds of prey centre with twice-daily flying displays. Up in the trees in spring are around 500 heron nests: a viewing tower gives what might be called a bird's-eye view. There's a farm and pets' pavilion, with animals that younger children can fuss over and stroke. Good play areas include an adventure playground and monkey slide for older children, and a new toddlers' play area in a fenced-off section next to the tearoom. A nice place to spend a couple of hours – perhaps longer with a picnic. Snacks, shop, disabled access; open daily Apr–Oct, wknds and school hols the rest of the year; (01603) 872274; £5.50 (£3.50

children 4–14). A family ticket (two adults and two children) is £16.

The riverside Fox & Hounds at nearby Lyng does good reasonably priced lunches, and there's an interesting pottery opposite it.

22. Dinosaur Park

(Weston Park, Lenwade, off A1067) A splendidly silly treat for small children, with life-size reconstructions of dinosaurs (inc a new tyrannosaurus) hidden in 300 acres of nicely kept woodland – good for children to see how big some of these beasts really were. Themed play areas (one specially for under-5s) include the ingenious Climb-a-Saurus, a 23-metre (75-ft) brontosaurus replica with slides, ladders and so on tucked away inside; also woodland maze, animals to handle, and other activities (for an extra charge) inc a deer safari, and crazy golf. Meals, snacks, shop, disabled access; open daily Easter–mid-Sept, plus Fri–Sun and school hols late Mar–Oct; (01603) 876312; £5.95 (£4.95 children 3–14). In Lenwade, the Bridge Inn has a good choice of well cooked food.

23. A parkland zoo

Banham Zoo (B1113, Banham) This well established and splendidly organised zoo is beautifully laid out, with over 1,000 animals spread over 35 acres of parkland. There's everything from kangaroos to crocodiles, with particularly good enclosures for their Siberian tigers and ring-tailed lemurs, and an underwater viewing window into Penguin World. A busy schedule of talks and feeding sessions is spread throughout the day, taking in fur seals, meerkats, tigers, and, in summer, twice-daily bird of prey displays. Children can wander among the guinea-pigs, miniature donkeys, goats and sheep in the Farm Barn, and there's an adventure play area. New animals are always popping up; recent additions include a Suffolk punch foal, a baby gibbon and a new female tiger – part of a European breeding programme; also recently added are a red panda enclosure and a vulture aviary. Meals, snacks, shops, disabled access; cl 25–26 Dec; (01953) 887771; £7.95. It's run by the same people as Suffolk Wildlife Park at Kessingland (see next page). Across the road are a few shops in the converted barns, of the Appleyard Craft Court, as well as a working cider mill. The Red Lion at nearby Kenninghall has enjoyable food.

24. Speedy rides, and 1930s trams and buses

Pleasurewood Hills Theme Park (off A12, Lowestoft) Lots of rides and family attractions to occupy a good bit of the day, inc a spinning roller-coaster; trains and chairlifts speed up travel around the grounds. Meals, snacks, shop, disabled access; open daily mid-May to mid-Sept, and wknds, bank hols and school hols Easter–Oct; (01502) 508200; £12.75.

East Anglia Transport Museum (Carlton Colville; B1384 SW of Lowestoft) Lots of lovingly restored vehicles around three acres of woodland. The best part is the reconstructed 1930s street scene used as a setting for working trams, trains and trolley-buses. Snacks, shop, some disabled access; open Easter, then Suns May–Sept, plus Weds and Sat pms Jun–Sept, and wkdy pms in summer hols; (01502) 518459; *£4.50. The nearby Crown (A146) does good cheap lunches.

Britain's most easterly town, Lowestoft is the area's main fishing port, so the harbour always has lots to see. It's developed as a resort thanks to its beaches (South Beach has the best bathing water) and proximity to the Broads. The seafront Jolly Sailors nr the quaint Pakefield church is good value for lunch.

25. Suffolk Wildlife Park

(A12, Kessingland) Quite an emphasis on African wildlife at this 100-acre park; some of the animals are the only examples of their type in the country – they've just got two very rare white rhinos. Lots for families in summer, inc a bouncy castle beside the play areas (with a new one for under-5s), animal feeding talks, bird of prey displays most days, crazy golf, and games and activities in summer hols. Feeding times are spread through the day. Meals, snacks, shop, disabled access; cl 25–26 Dec; (01502) 740291; £7.50. Kessingland's beach is good, though busy in summer, and it's only three or four miles to Lowestoft.

26. A vintage working farm, with plenty of fun

Easton Farm Park (Easton) With 35 acres of attractive countryside, there are plenty of opportunities for children to get close to the animals at this delightful working farm, and as well as poultry, Suffolk horses, pigs and goats, there are usually some young animals. Pony rides are included in the price (they usually have them at wknds and school hols), and you can watch milking displays every afternoon in the modern dairy (2–3.30). There's a good play area, as well as token-operated battery-powered tractors, and a full-size one to scramble over. Other activities include a working blacksmith, face-painting, environmental trail and vintage farm machinery. Dogs are welcome if kept on a lead; the gravel paths can be tricky in places for pushchairs. Snacks, picnic areas, shop; cl Mon (exc bank hols and in July and Aug), and all Oct to mid-Mar (exc half-terms); (01728) 746475; £4.75. The quaint White Horse has decent food, and the Wickham Market–Debenham road through here via Brandeston and Cretingham has some attractive views.

27. How people used to live

Museum of East Anglian Life (Iliffe Way, opp Asda, Stowmarket) This excellent 70-acre open-air museum may not be the first place that springs to mind when planning a family day out, but children who've been on school trips here often come back with their parents, so it's clearly somewhere younger visitors appreciate. They look at the reconstructed buildings with a genuine sense of astonishment (did people really live like that?), and even the 1950s domestic room settings seem prehistoric to fresher eyes. Most of the buildings have been removed from their original settings and rebuilt here; the oldest is a splendid 13th-c timber barn, now housing a collection of horse-drawn vehicles. Among the rest are an old schoolroom, a smithy, chapel, windpump, and a very pretty watermill. They're quite spread out, so a fair bit of walking is involved, inc a nice stroll down by the river. Also wandering around are various traditional farm animals, and on Sun they often have demonstrations of local crafts and skills like wood-turning and basket-making, some of which you can join in; it's worth checking what's going on. They have occasional event days with extra children's activities, usually around the spring and summer bank hols. There's a decent rustic-style adventure play area, and plenty of space to run around. The museum's not ideal for under-5s, and teenagers might not find it that exciting (unless they like history), but otherwise in fine weather families can spend anything between two hours and a very relaxing full day here; it's great for a picnic. Dogs are welcome on a lead. They have a big firework display around Bonfire Night. Snacks, shop, disabled access; cl Nov–Mar; (01449) 612229; £4.50 adults, £3 children 4–16. The family ticket only really saves you money if you bring three children; it's £14.75.

Over at Buxhall the Crown has good food, and its pretty garden has a play area and heated terrace.

28. Unusual stately home, set out well for children

Ickworth House, Park and Gardens (Horringer) Very untypical stately home, an oval rotunda 30 metres (98 ft) high, with two curved corridors filled with a fascinating art collection inc pictures by Gainsborough, and an exceptional array of Georgian silver. They try hard to make sure children enjoy their visit, with quizzes, trails, handling boxes and a free touch tour, introduced primarily for partially sighted visitors. Outside are formal Italianate gardens, and 1,800 acres of attractive parkland with woodland walks and cycle routes. There's a decent-sized play area, special events and activities for children, and themed events in the run-up to Christmas. Meals, snacks, shop, plant centre, good disabled access; house open pms (exc Mon and Thurs) Apr–Sept; garden cl winter wknds; park open all year; (01284) 735270; £5.70 house, park and garden; £2.50 park and gardens only; NT.

The serenely attractive village has a good dining pub the Beehive.

29. Time-travel to the 1940s – or even 1600

Kentwell Hall (Long Melford) Beautiful Tudor mansion with genuinely friendly lived-in feel, best during their enthusiastic re-creations of Elizabethan and 1940s life (several wknds Apr–Sept), when everything is done as close as possible to the way it would have been done then – even the speech. It's surrounded by a broad moat, and there's a rare breeds farm within the grounds. Snacks, shop, disabled access; house open Sun pm Mar–Oct, Easter week, and daily mid-July to late Sept; (01787) 310207; most re-creations cost around £8.50, though the Great Annual one is £12. On non-event days entry is £5.70, or £3.60 garden and farm only.

The Bull Hotel, one of the finer old buildings in this beautiful village, does good light lunches, as does the comfortable Black Lion

Hotel; the Crown, Cock & Bell and Hare are also useful for food, and there are plenty of interesting antiques shops.

30. Animal rescue, nuclear refuge

Environmental & Animal Centre (New Rd, Mistley) Very friendly animal rescue centre: Ping and Pong the Vietnamese pot-bellied pigs may come to greet you as you go in. Snacks (not summer Mons, wknds only in winter), shop, disabled access; (01206) 396483; £2.50. The village has the remains of a Robert Adam church (known locally as the Mistley Towers). If you come by train, don't miss the splendid station buffet at Manningtree; the Crown in the High St there, with a conservatory overlooking the Stour estuary, has a good choice of family food.

    Essex Secret Bunker (B1352, Mistley) Much of its original equipment has been returned by Government agencies and other groups, so the operations centre at this nuclear war command centre looks especially authentic. Odd seeing something so contemporary consigned to history, especially when similar establishments are still in operation. Snacks, shop, disabled access; open wknds 5 Jan–24 Feb, daily 2 Mar–27 Oct, and maybe at other times, phone to check; (01206) 392271; *£4.95.

31. Europe's biggest Norman castle keep

Colchester Castle Museum (Castle Park, off High St) Ideal for families: they let you try on Roman togas and helmets, or touch 2,000-year-old pottery excavated nearby; also splendid collection of Roman relics from jewellery to military tombstones. The castle itself has the biggest Norman keep in Europe, and stands on the site of a colossal Roman temple (you can still see the vaults). They go to some lengths to bring grisly moments in its history to life:

you can hear a dramatisation of one of the forced confessions of the suspect witches incarcerated here. For £1.25 extra a guided castle tour takes you up on the roof as well as to the vaults and chapel. Good shop, mostly disabled access (to castle museum but not to vaults or castle roof); cl 25–26 Dec and 1 Jan; (01206) 282939; £3.90.

Hollytrees Museum (High St) Now much more appealing to families, with hands-on and audio displays, this Georgian town house has recently reopened following lottery-funded improvements. There are new displays on its history and famous local figures, as well as the existing collection of toys, costumes and curios from the last two centuries. Shop, disabled access; cl 25–26 Dec and 1 Jan; (01206) 282940; free.

The capital of Roman Britain, Colchester is Britain's oldest recorded town. You can trace the Roman wall (the Hole in the Wall, Balkerne Gdns, is a decent pub built into the one surviving fragmentary gatehouse). The Tudor Rose & Crown (East St) is good for lunch.

32. Colchester Zoo

(Maldon Rd, Stanway, 2m E of Colchester by B1002) One of the country's most satisfying animal collections, with over 200 rare and endangered species kept in enclosures as close to their natural environment as possible – several splendidly improved in recent years, with cheetahs, penguins, chimps, giraffes and tigers among those finding themselves in smart new homes. The zoo is particularly good on cats and primates, but one enclosure has shire horses, pigs, rabbits and other tame animals for children to get close to; they hope to add warthogs and a vulture aviary over the next few months. Several good play areas (our favourite is the Kalahari Capers under-cover complex), and an activity centre with changing animal-related or Native American crafts; activities such as face-painting and brass-rubbing included in the price. Meals, snacks, shops, indoor and outdoor picnic areas, mostly disabled access; cl 25 Dec; (01206) 331292; £8.80 (£5.60 children 3–14). You can save up to £1.30 off the normal adult price by booking more than 48 hours in advance on their website, www.colchester-zoo.co.uk; the tickets stay valid for a year.

33. A day out in Southend

Central Museum & Planetarium (Victoria Ave) The only planetarium in the South-East outside London, with a local history museum and a hands-on discovery centre. Shop; cl Sun, Mon, inc bank hols (planetarium cl Sun–Tues); (01702) 215131; planetarium £2.25, museum and discovery centre free.

    Sea Life Adventure (Eastern Esplanade) The highlight is the walk-through tunnel along a reconstructed sea bed with sharks; you can watch shoals of piranhas being fed, and there are regular daily talks. Meals, snacks, shop, disabled access; cl 25 Dec; (01702) 462400; £4.95. Also here is a new three-storey children's play centre (£3 or joint ticket £5.50, adults free).

    Southchurch Hall Museum (Park Lane) An unexpected find, a medieval moated manor house in an attractive park, with period room settings, and fun talks on Tudor life; occasional lute demonstrations. Shop, limited disabled access; cl Sun and Mon, bank hols, and over Christmas and Easter; (01702) 467671; free (small charge for talks).

    Southend is a traditional seaside resort long favoured by East Londoners, with many of the attractions you'd expect to find. Most famous is the pier, the longest in the world, excellent for fishing, with a museum (open wknds, Tues–Weds and bank hols) and happily a restored train service – it's a long walk there and back.

Like many such resorts, Southend in winter has a special appeal for people who wouldn't like it in summer – seafront shops by the endless promenade looking closed for ever, the sea itself a doleful muddy grey. Adjoining Leigh-on-Sea has a quite distinct character, altogether more intimate, with wood-clad buildings and shrimp boats in the working harbour; Ivy Osborne's cockle stall here is justly famous.

34. Nuclear war and country life

Barleylands Farm Museum & Visitor Centre (A129 SE of Billericay) Expanding series of attractions, from farm animals and rural life displays to working glassworks, craft studios and miniature railway (summer Sun and daily in Aug), also picnic and play areas. Meals, snacks, shop, disabled access; cl Nov–Feb; (01268) 290229; £3.50. The nearby Duke of York (South Green) has good value food.

   Secret Nuclear Bunker (Kelvedon Hatch, off A128) Who'd have thought that a three-storey Cold War underground complex lay beneath this innocuous 1950s bungalow? Knowledgeable tours take you through all parts of this clinically self-sufficient little world, and are done with real relish, but you can't help feeling relieved when you're back in the surrounding woodland. Wknd meals, snacks, shop; cl Mon–Weds Nov–Feb and 25 Dec; (01277) 364883; *£5. The Black Horse in Pilgrims Hatch is another good handy dining pub.

35. Gunpowder and country life

Royal Gunpowder Mills (Beaulieu Drive, Powdermill Lane, off A121 just W of Waltham Abbey) Interesting newly opened place, showing the evolution of gunpowder technology, the impact it has had on history, and what it was like to work in the gunpowder mills. There's a short film, and plenty of hands-on and interactive displays – children can try on a millworkers' clothes, help design a bouncing bomb and listen to the stories of past millworkers. Many of the restored buildings are now open, and larger displays include a powder boat and a railway locomotive. There are plenty of walks around the 175-acre site (you can also pick up various children's activity sheets), and land train tours take you through the places not accessible on foot. A good place for wildlife, with muntjac deer, otters and the largest colony of herons in the county. Meals, shop, disabled access; cl Nov-Apr; (01992) 707370; £5.90.

Lee Valley Park Farms (B194, 2m N of Waltham Abbey) Takes in Hayes Hill children's farm with plenty of traditional animals, a pet centre and play area, and Holyfield Hall working farm and dairy, with 150 cows milked every afternoon around 3pm, and seasonal events such as sheep-shearing and harvesting. Meals, snacks, shop, disabled access; (01992) 892781; *£3.10.

36. Toys galore in action, and a lively Norman castle

House on the Hill Toy Museum (Grove Hill, Stansted) The biggest privately owned toy museum in Europe, with over 30,000 amazingly varied playthings from Victorian times to the present. As well as fascinating aged tin soldiers and dolls, all the favourites are here: Hornby trains, Dinky and Corgi models, Action Man – and a good selection of teddy bears. What's particularly nice is that while quite a few toy museums appeal more to adults than children, here they've made a real effort to make the displays entertaining for all ages. Many are animated, so you see the soldiers, trains and Meccano in action (though, sadly, no catfight between Barbie and rival Sindy). There are a few coin-operated slot machines, puppet shows, plenty of TV memorabilia, and a good collectors' shop:

they're always ready to buy new (old) toys if you're clearing out the loft. Cl Christmas week; (01279) 813237; £3.80 adults, £2.80 children.

Five minutes' walk down the hill and run by the same people is the intriguing **Mountfitchet Castle**, an authentically reconstructed Norman castle and village, complete with thatched houses, herb gardens, church, catapult to repel marauding invaders, and deer, sheep, goats and chickens wandering between them. Near the castle is a small chunk of the original. Though there are days when you'll see period re-enactments, they're not the norm: most villagers are fairly static dummies, in sufficiently gruesome positions to delight younger visitors, particularly around the prison (older children won't find them as convincing). You can buy food to feed the animals, many of which have been rescued after accidents or ill-treatment. Cheerful and enthusiastic rather than sophisticated, it's an excellent introduction to life a thousand years ago, though you will need to visit on a dry day (the Toy Museum is all indoors, so good in any weather). No smoking around the castle. Snacks (and space for picnics), shop, disabled access; cl mid-Nov to mid-Mar; telephone as above; £4.80 adults (£3.80 children). If you visit both on the same day you'll save 10% off the entry price.

37. Furry fun for younger children

Paradise Wildlife Park (White Stubbs Lane, Broxbourne) Younger children should find plenty to keep them amused at this friendly little zoo and leisure park, which seems to grow and add new things every year. New residents include Brazilian tapirs and red pandas, but a particularly popular recent addition has nothing to do with living animals at all: it's a small woodland railway that runs past big fibreglass models of dinosaurs. There's a busy schedule of live shows and displays, from their jolly themed parrot displays to feeding the lions and cheetahs (usually quite late in the afternoon, but a highlight worth staying for). Children can feed the camels, zebra and other creatures in the paddocks, and go right up to the usual farmyard animals. Also, a good collection of bugs and creepy-crawlies, falconry displays and undemanding rides and amusements inc a bouncy castle, slides, helter-skelter, roundabouts, and a paddling pool. Older children won't find it so exciting, though there is crazy golf. Most of it's outdoors, so better in fine weather. Meals, snacks, shop, disabled access; open every day, inc Christmas Day (no shows then, and they don't charge for entry); (01992) 468001; £8 adults, £6 children 2–15.

38. Knebworth House

(Old Knebworth) The splendid house at the centre of this 250-acre park was originally a straightforward Tudor mansion, but was spectacularly embellished for Victorian author Sir Edward Bulwer-Lytton; he wanted it to be a castle fit for the romantic characters in his novels. Still a lived-in home (the same family has been here for over 500 years), the grand rooms include a splendid Jacobean great hall, a display on the great days of the Raj, and mementos of former guests like Dickens and Churchill. The well restored gardens were designed by Lutyens, and include a herb garden laid out to plans by Gertrude Jekyll, and a newly designed walled garden; there's also a deer park, a maze, and a miniature railway. There's an exceptionally good adventure playground – in addition to the usual wooden climbing equipment and so forth there are quite a few exciting slides, inc the monorail suspension slide, and the twisting Corkscrew, plus a separate enclosure for younger children. Lots of special events through the year. Meals, snacks, shop, limited disabled access; open wknds Easter–Sept, daily early July–early Sept and during school hols but best to check; house open only in the afternoons; (01438) 812661; £7 for everything (£6.50 children 4–16) – £5.50 grounds only. Along the outer edge of the park is the pretty little hamlet of Old Knebworth; the Lytton Arms, which does good value food, welcomes children in its restaurant.

39. A farm geared to children

Standalone Farm (Wilbury Rd, Letchworth) This farm has got something of an educational bent, so appeals most to younger children with a genuine interest in animals, who'll get an unaffected look at life and activities down on the farm. Spring is definitely the best time to come, when you'll find new-born calves, chicks and other animals, and can watch the lambs being bottle-fed. Plenty of animals to enjoy the rest of the year too, from shire horse and Shetland ponies to rabbits, chipmunks and guinea-pigs. Pigs, free-range chickens and rare breeds of poultry wander around the farmyard, and there are paddocks of sheep and goats. Two friendly Jersey cows take part in milking demonstrations every day at 2.30 (1.30 during school term). An exhibition farm has a working beehive, model dinosaurs and various creepy-crawlies, and there's an outdoor play area next to a decent spot for picnics. There are picnic areas indoors too, and most animals and displays are under cover on a wet day. Children can also climb on Fergie, a red static play tractor, and there are 170 acres of farmland to explore, with walks and an arboretum. Snacks, shop, disabled access; open daily Mar–Sept, and Oct half-term; (01462) 686775; £2.95 (£1.90 children over 3).

40. Falconry, historic aeroplanes and a swiss garden

English School of Falconry (splendidly positioned in the grounds of Shuttleworth Mansion, Old Warden) They have more than 300 birds in settings close to their natural surroundings in this new Birds of Prey Centre inc the rare king vulture, crested seriema and brahminy kite. There are daily talks and flying demonstrations (10.30, 12.30, 2.30, plus 4 in summer) as well as the chance to hold a bird; lots of aviaries inc the walk-through barn where the owls are free to fly around you. Meals, snacks, shop, disabled access; cl 25–26 Dec, 1 Jan; (01767) 627527; £6.

Shuttleworth Collection Nearly 40 working historic aeroplanes covering the early history of aviation, from 1909 Bleriot to 1942 Spitfire in purpose-built hangars on a classic grass aerodrome. Several exhibits are the only surviving examples of their type, and it's worth trying to go on one on the days when some of them are flown (usually the first Sun of the month and Sat evenings, May– Oct; best to phone). Meals, snacks, shop, disabled access; cl Christmas wk; (01767) 627288; £6.

Swiss Garden Early 19th-c romantic wilderness garden is a nice place for a wander, with pretty vistas and colourful trees and shrubs. Meals, snacks, shop, disabled access; open Sun and bank hols Jan–Oct, plus pm daily Mar–Sept; (01767) 627666; £3. Now approached from Old Warden Park via Shuttleworth Mansion.

You can get a triple ticket which includes all three attractions for £12.50. Old Warden is an attractive village in its own right, built deliberately quaintly in the 19th c. The village church has a number of European wood carvings, inc some from the private chapel of Henry VIII's wife Anne of Cleves. The White Horse at Southill and Crown at Northill are both nearby family dining pubs with great play areas (the White Horse sometimes has a miniature diesel train working); the Cock at Broom is a really classic country pub which also takes children.

41. Outstanding stately home and safari park

Woburn Abbey & Deer Park One of England's grandest stately homes – everything from the lovely English and French 18th-c furniture to the splendid range of silver seems to have the edge over most assemblages elsewhere, and the art collection, taking in sumptuous paintings by Rembrandt, Van Dyck and Gainsborough, is outstanding (where else can you see 21 Canalettos in just one room?) The 3,000 acres of surrounding parkland were landscaped by Humphrey Repton, and today are home to several varieties of deer. Swans, ducks and other waterfowl on the lake; pottery and huge antiques centre. Meals, snacks, shop, disabled access by arrangement; cl Nov–Dec and wkdys Oct and Jan–Mar; (01525) 290666; £7.50. The attractive drive into the park through Froxfield has masses of rhododendrons in June.

Woburn Safari Park Always exciting, the highlight here is the drive-through safari – you can almost imagine you are driving through African plains, with lions and tigers (if you're lucky) just on the other side of the windscreen – pick your day carefully though: bank hols can produce slow-moving traffic jams, so it's probably best to avoid coming then. The 300 acres of parkland also feature giraffes, rhinos, bears, sea lion, penguin feeding and elephant shows, animal encounters, a train ride, a toboggan run and a boating lake. Birds swoop down and feed from your hand in a walk-through aviary, and a new woodland walk takes you among friendly wallabies. Meals, snacks, shop, disabled access; cl wkdys Nov–Feb; (01525) 290407; £12.50 (£9 children, free for under-3s in cars); 50p extra in July–Aug.

42. Crafts, carriages and countryside

Stockwood Craft Museum & Gardens (Stockwood Country Park, Farley Hill, Luton) Ideal for a restrained and uncomplicated day out. Besides a museum and several lovely period garden settings (inc a 17th-c knot garden and a Victorian cottage garden), there's a refreshingly witty sculpture garden, and an adjacent children's play area. Also here, the **Mossman Collection** concentrates on the history of horse-drawn transport from Roman times onwards with more than 70 vehicles – the Royal Mail coach is particularly noteworthy. Snacks, shop, disabled access; cl Mon (exc bank hols), wkdys Nov–Mar, 25–26 Dec, 1 Jan; (01582) 738714; free.

Dunstable Downs Very popular with kite-fliers and gliders at wknds or in summer, and a super spot for picnics; there's a countryside centre (cl Mon exc summer school hols, and winter wkdys), two car parks, and lots of space to run around. The downs give great views from a spectacular escarpment path, amid ancient grasslands. For families that like hearty walks, the downs can be linked to a circuit incorporating Whipsnade village and the nearby Tree Cathedral (see next entry). This is the best walk in the county. The Horse & Jockey (A5183) is a useful family food pub.

43. Whipsnade Wild Animal Park

Whipsnade Easy to spot by the big chalk lion carved into the hillside, this enormous place has plenty of space for its huge range of animals – and for families and children to explore. You'll easily need a full day to see everything, and it's too big to get around completely on foot; an open topped tour bus can take you between the various stopping points, but it's more fun on their narrow gauge railway, which chuffs past herds of Asian animals. You can usually drive your own vehicle round the perimeter road and walk from designated parking areas, but as we went to press cars still weren't allowed as a continued precaution against Foot and Mouth. Altogether 2,500 animals roam the beautiful downs-edge parkland, from tigers, giraffes and rhinos, to monkeys, wallabies, peafowl and Chinese water deer; last year they added a 96-ft aviary. Their 17-acre elephant paddock is the biggest in

Europe. As you'd expect, there are several daily demonstrations: most popular are the penguin feeding displays and sealion shows – bag your seat fast for the sealions, though not too near the front (unless you want to get wet). Check the times carefully, as some displays can clash. Younger children will find plenty to keep them happy and interested: there's a hands-on children's farm, a big adventure playground, and a few smaller activities linked to the animals on the way round. You'll get more out of the park by visiting on a dry day, though there is an indoor discovery centre, with dwarf crocodiles, snakes and spiders. Whipsnade has an excellent record in conservation and breeding: last year they welcomed baby rhinos and several rare baby camels. Their successes have led to several species being saved from extinction, and in some instances they've been able to reintroduce them to the wild. Meals, snacks, disabled access; cl 25 Dec; (01582) 872171; £10.70 adults, £8 children 3–15; it's an extra £2 for the main car park.

The Farmers Boy at Kensworth (B4540, Whipsnade end) is a nearby family dining pub that's really welcoming to children. And you might like to look in on the Tree Cathedral, just off the Whipsnade village road: most unusual, trees planted in the shape of a cathedral.

44. Gulliver's Land

(Newlands, Milton Keynes, nr M1 junction 14) Most under-12s will happily spend a day at this friendly family-run place. Like its sister parks at Matlock Bath and Warrington, it's loosely based on Jonathan Swift's tale of the shipwrecked surgeon taken prisoner by the pint-sized population of Lilliput. Most of the 30 or so rides and attractions are scaled-down versions of what you'd expect, but there are some unusual ones: you can travel on musical instruments and flying boots, or on a water ride that whisks you through waterfalls and whirlpools; good play area for the under-5s. Most rides are under cover; special events, restaurants, cafés, shops, disabled access; open wknds Easter–Jun and daily Jun–mid-Sept – may be best to ring outside peak summer times; (01908) 609001; £8.80 adults and children, includes unlimited goes on everything all day. Free for children under 90cm (they may not be able to go on some rides).

45. From goats and donkeys to Willy Wonka

Bucks Goat Centre (Layby Farm, just off A4010 nr Stoke Mandeville) Goats galore as well as a pig, poultry, pony, donkeys and pets; you can feed the animals (they sell bags of cut-up vegetables in the shop). Many animals are under cover, so good for a rainy day. Also farm shop (with cheese and fudge made from goat's milk), and various others inc a specialist Korean furniture shop. Meals, snacks, disabled access; cl Mon (exc bank hols); (01296) 612983; *£3.

Buckinghamshire County Museum and Roald Dahl Children's Gallery (St Mary's Sq, Church St, Aylesbury) Roald Dahl lived in Buckinghamshire for most of his life, and as well as having local history displays, this museum celebrates the connection with a gallery of hands-on displays that use Dahl's novels and characters to teach children about insects, light and any number of other topics; visitors can crawl through the tunnel of Fantastic Mr Fox, discover Willy Wonka's inventions, and even go inside the Giant Peach to find out what things look like under the microscope. Also a good collection of regional art and a walled garden. Snacks, shop, good disabled access; cl Sun am and 25–26 Dec (Dahl gallery cl until 3pm wkdys in term-time); (01296) 331441; £3.50 (inc free entry to main museum).

Nearby, the recently reopened Kings Head, owned by the National Trust, is an almost unique Tudor inn around a courtyard, with a small crafts shop in the corner.

46. Intriguing collection of bygone buildings

Chiltern Open-Air Museum (Newland Park, Gorelands Lane, Chalfont St Giles) A good few traditional Chilterns buildings that would otherwise have been demolished have found their way here in the last 20 years or so, painstakingly dismantled and rebuilt again piece by piece. Dotted about the 45 acres are structures as diverse as an Iron Age house, a Victorian farmyard, an Edwardian public convenience and a 1940s prefab, with useful displays on their original use; also a pretty woodland walk (best in May when the bluebells are out), and a children's playground. Hands-on activities most days, and special events on some bank hols (may have extra charges). Snacks and picnic area, shop, some disabled access; open Apr–Oct; (01494) 872163; £5.50 (£3 children 5–16). Nearby, the smart Ivy House (London Rd) has good food.

47. A farm that's great for younger children

Odds Farm Park (Wooburn Common) Just about all farms appeal most to their younger visitors, but that's especially the case with this well organised old favourite, where everything has been carefully designed with children in mind. They can go right up to the cattle, pigs, sheep and poultry, and join in daily activities such as bottle-feeding the lambs, hand-milking the goats, or collecting the chickens' eggs. Quite a bit of effort has gone into the outdoor and indoor play areas (one of which is specially for under-5s), and most pens and enclosures have signs written in a way that children can understand. Each month there are weekend events with a different theme; from lambing in March and sheepdog demonstrations in April, to cart-rides in July and September and pumpkin carving in October. They may have puppet shows at weekends in November, and Father Christmas calls in most weekends in December. You could also come across tractor and trailer rides in summer, and even occasional donkey rides. At any time, children can pet the rabbits and guinea pigs, while older ones can learn a lot about farm life: they work hard to make sure the displays are instructive as well as fun. Usefully, it's just as good in winter, when everything takes place under cover (the animals are in barns and sheds then). There are some days when not every activity will take place, so best to check first if there's something you're particularly keen to do. Plenty of space for picnics. Not an enormous place, it's all the better for not being overly developed, and children find it an endless source of fascination. Snacks, shop, disabled access; cl 25–26 Dec, and Mon–Weds from mid-Nov to Feb; (01628) 520188; £4.25 adults, £3.25 children over 2.

Nearby Burnham Beeches is a supreme example of a Chilterns beechwood, splendid in spring and autumn colours, and with maybe a glimpse of deer. There are lovely spots for picnics here. Maps are posted throughout the forest, but it is quite easy to lose one's bearings. The main starting-point is at East Burnham Common car park, opposite the W end of Beeches Rd at Farnham Common.

48. Blenheim Palace

(Woodstock) One of England's most impressive stately homes: given to the Duke of Marlborough by Queen Anne as a reward for his military achievements, the house itself covers 14 acres, and the grounds stretch for well over 2,000. Churchill was born here, and there's a straightforward exhibition on his life. Highlights within the palace include the sumptuous State Rooms and 56-metre (183-ft) Long Library, along with plenty of opulent furnishings and sculpture; tours leave every 5–10 minutes. The very extensive grounds, landscaped by Capability Brown, are full of interesting paths and tracks; you can take a picnic. Also butterfly house, miniature railway and play areas with swings, ropes and slides. An extra £1.50 adds a hedge maze, putting green, and model village based on Woodstock and surroundings. You can arrange coarse fishing on the lake (phone first to book). There's enough space to absorb the crowds (Sun is busiest, and Weds is popular with overseas students). Meals and snacks (three different restaurants), several shops and plant centre, some disabled access; house cl Nov to mid-Mar, grounds open all yr; (01993) 811325; £9.50, £6 per car grounds only. There is also a public right of way through the huge estate, with pleasant walks, for example from the attractive village of Combe.

In Woodstock the Queens Own (food all day wknds), stream-side Black Prince (armour and swords) and grander Feathers are all good for meals, with attractive gardens or courtyards.

49. Victorian country life

Cogges Farm Museum (Church Lane, Witney) This charming old place gives a useful illustration of rural life in Victorian times. Most popular with children are the demonstrations of cooking in the Victorian kitchen; 'maids' in period costume let you sample old-fashioned cakes and biscuits, and explain how they managed in the days when even the kitchen sink was a far-off luxury. The striking manor house dates back seven centuries in parts; there are taped tours of the upstairs rooms, and an activity room with Victorian toys and games. Younger visitors can usually try on period clothes. Outside are the sorts of animals you'd have found on the farm 100 years ago: shire horses, pigs, cows, chickens and turkeys, with regular feeding displays, and hand-milking in the old dairy. On some days they have weaving, spinning, lace-making or butter-making demonstrations. The grounds are attractive, with walled gardens, a riverside walk and a peaceful orchard. Some displays seem a little outdated (dummies in corners and roped-off exhibits) but staff are knowledgeable and work hard to keep up everyone's enthusiasm. There's a good calendar of seasonal events. Meals, snacks, shop, mostly disabled access; open daily exc Mon end Mar–Oct; (01993) 772602; £4.20.

Witney, quiet and relaxed, was a prosperous town in the Middle Ages. There are quite a few interesting and picturesque old buildings such as the 13th-c church and 18th-c blanket hall (it's always been famous for its blankets), and the market square still has its ancient butter cross and 17th-c clock. Just off Church Green you can see the excavated foundations of a 12th-c palace of the Bishops of Winchester (pm wknds Easter-mid Sept, free). The Three Horseshoes (Corn St) has good food.

Nearby Minster Lovell is well worth an after-lunch wander. One of the prettiest and most unspoilt old villages in the area, it has an attractive 15th-c church, village green, and 15th-c bridge over the River Windrush narrow enough for the Welsh drovers to use for counting the sheep in the flocks they brought this way each year. Imposing and attractively set, Minster Lovell Hall was being used as ramshackle farm buildings until its restoration as neat ruins in the 1930s. Macabre stories about the 15th-c Hall usually involve people being shut up in various places and forgotten about until their skeletons are discovered much later. Open every day, free. There's a well restored medieval dovecot nearby.

50. Cotswold Wildlife Park

(Bradwell Grove, nr Burford; A361, 2m S of junction with A40) No problem in keeping children happy for most of the day at this big place, well liked by readers, and pretty much unchallenged in this county for the mantle of best family day out. One of the things that makes it so special is the way it's been so attractively laid out in the grounds of a gothick manor house. It's spread over 160 acres of the estate's gardens and parkland, and even parts of the house have been nicely adapted: the former stables and outbuildings are now a reptile house and Bat Belfry, and the old dining room is an animal-themed brass-rubbing centre. Hundreds of different animals range from flamingos and ostriches through apes, zebras and the delightful red panda, to lions, cheetahs and rhinos, all in spacious re-creations of their natural environment (they have an excellent track record with breeding). Peacocks wander freely around the grounds. Everything's well signposted and labelled, so you always have a good idea of where you're going and what you're looking at. They have various animal encounters and feeding displays throughout the day; as ever, the penguin feeding times are among the most popular. A children's farmyard has the usual petting opportunities, and there's a good adventure playground (with an old-fashioned carousel in summer). A narrow-gauge railway operates Apr–Oct (£1 extra). As well as the animals outside, there's a tropical house (plenty of interesting plants, as well as colourfully exotic birds), insect and butterfly house, and a 49-metre (160-ft) walk-through aviary. Plenty of space for picnics: several shelters are under cover. Some summer wknds they may have birds of prey displays, and there's a grotto in the run-up to Christmas. Dogs on a lead allowed in some areas. Meals and snacks, shops (one specially for children), disabled access; cl 25 Dec; (01993) 823006; £6.50 adults, £4 children 3–16.

Besides the many places to eat in the lovely village of Burford itself, there's good home-made food from sandwiches up at the Rose & Crown opposite the pond over in Shilton; and the rather smart Five Alls does good meals, off the A361 further along at Filkins. There, Cotswold Woollen Weavers is a friendly working woollen mill, with demonstrations of traditional production methods in 18th-c buildings. Snacks, well stocked shop, some disabled access; (01367) 860491; cl am Sun, 25-31 Dec; free.

51. Legoland

(B3022, 2m SW of Windsor centre; shuttle-bus from the station at Windsor & Eton Riverside, which connects with London Waterloo) Ever-expanding and truly imaginative, Legoland is one of the most visited attractions in Britain: to miss the long wait at the entrance, booking in advance is a good idea. Divided into several differently themed areas, highlights include the driving school at Lego Traffic, the Rat Trap – a first-class labyrinth of wooden walkways, climbing nets and slides – and an excellent steep water chute. Children over nine can create robotic models in the more sophisticated Mindstorms Centre (entrance is by timed ticket, so try and sort out your slot as soon as you arrive). The colourful Duplo Gardens appeal to younger children, while My Town has some jolly fairground rides and a circus; there's a virtual reality racing game, but best of all is Miniland, where 32 million Lego bricks charmingly re-create European capitals in miniature, with moving people, vehicles and animals, and wonderful attention to detail. You'll need a full day to stand even a chance of seeing everything (it stays open later in the summer holidays); a two-day ticket (£7 extra) helps to avoid rushing. Meals, snacks, shops, good disabled access; open daily 9 Mar–3 Nov; (08705) 040404; £19 (£16 children). Be warned – they close the doors when they feel there are enough visitors.

52. Look Out

(3m from Bracknell centre, well signed; Nine Mile Ride, off B3430) This busy centre should satisfy both lively minds and legs. It's the starting point for 2,600 acres of woodland, but the main feature is the under-cover hands-on science centre. Visitors can enjoy climbing through a giant mole hole, try the Puzzle Carousel, or have a go at launching a miniature hydrogen rocket or hot-air balloon. Mainly conifer plantations, the forest is full of nature trails and wildlife; you can hire mountain bikes (school hols and wknds only (01344) 874611; £8 for two hours), the many tracks, some based on Roman roads, allow long if not varied walks and rides (one leading to an Iron Age hill fort). There are good views from the 22-metre look-out tower, and plenty of picnic places. Meals, snacks, shop, disabled access; cl 25–26 Dec; (01344) 354400; £3.95 (half price after 4 o'clock, but shuts at 5). For those with any energy left, across the road the Coral Reef swimming pool complex is great for younger members of the family; the Wild Water Rapids are the best bit (cl 2 wks before Christmas; (01344) 862525; £5.50).

53. Country life then and now

Museum of English Rural Life (Univ of Reading, Whiteknights Park; 2m SE on A327, so you don't have to go into the busy centre – though a new multi-million pound grant will eventually put them in new premises there) You won't find a better exploration of life in the English countryside over the last couple of centuries than this, taking in farm tools, rural crafts, and domestic room settings. Shop, disabled access; cl 1–2pm, all day Sun and Mon, and 25 Dec–1 Jan; (0118) 931 8661; *£1.

Keeping on down the A327 then turning off on the B3272 into Eversley centre, you pass the Golden Pot, a cheerful well run pub with very enjoyable food. From here, an interesting drive is along the B3348, passing first the Finchampstead Ridges (National Trust heathland, pleasant for strolls), then an avenue of gigantic wellingtonia trees. At the end of the avenue, turn left on to the A321, then right on to the B3430 (the Nine Mile Ride, dead straight for that distance), then first proper left into Heathlands Rd.

Holme Grange Craft Village (Heathlands Rd, just SE of Wokingham) Craft centre with paintings, sculpture, rugs, traditional sweets and even a circus shop; Widget the pot-bellied pig is a favourite with children, and they've now got chipmunks and an aviary. Snacks, shops, disabled access; cl 25 Dec–1 Jan; (0118) 977 6753; free. Heathlands Rd has a couple of farm shops and pick-your-own plots; the nearby Crooked Billet (Honey Hill) is a friendly place for lunch.

If there's still some energy to unleash, go back along the B3430 to the California Country Park, nr Wick Hill. These woods and open spaces are very useful for young children to let off steam in.

54. Traditional farm visit

Bucklebury Farm Park (on the edge of Bucklebury, signed from Hermitage off A34) This notably friendly little farm park is a good bet for under-12s who are into animals. Attractively set in the Pang Valley, it's fairly unspoilt and unsophisticated – a good, traditional farm with all the animals you'd expect, plus, more unusually, a big herd of red deer. A tractor-drawn trailer ride (included in the price) takes you right up to them, and some are even tame enough to feed. June is perhaps the best time to come, when the deer calves are born, but there's plenty going on the rest of the time: children can bottle feed lambs and calves in spring, and handle rabbits and guinea pigs in the pets corner. It's a nice spot for simply ambling round – they own five acres of woodland (awash with bluebells in spring), and there's a two-mile way-marked walk across an ancient common. There's a decent enclosed adventure playground with climbing frames and a castle, and a cable slide for slightly older children. Their pick-your-own strawberries have been popular, but last season weren't available. As with most farms, you can easily be in and out in a couple of hours, or stretch it out much longer with walks and a picnic. Snacks, disabled access, cl Nov–mid-Mar; (0118) 971 4002; £3.50 adults, £2.50 children over 3.

In the village the Blade Bone (Chapel Row) has a wide choice of good food; they do children's helpings, and the garden has a play area.

55. Steam City

Steam (Kemble Drive, Swindon, next to the well signed Great Western Designer Outlet Centre) In the former works of the Great Western Railway, this brings to life the sights and sounds of the railway age, with good reconstructions. At the railway's peak 12,000 people worked here to produce everything needed to keep it running; you can see several of the locomotives built here. Particularly good fun is a simulator that re-creates the experience of riding on a steam train footplate, but there's as much emphasis on the people who worked and travelled on the railways as there is on the trains. Plenty to keep children amused, from the various touch-screen games and hands-on activities to a track layout where younger visitors have fun shunting the trucks. Other displays focus on Isambard Kingdom Brunel and the GWR's days as the 'holiday line', and you can watch restoration work on old engines and carriages. This has much wider appeal than many steam-themed collections, and all ages seem to get something out of it; good special events. Meals, snacks, shop, disabled access; cl 25–26 Dec; (01793) 466646; £5.70. There are lots of bargains at the outlet shopping centre next door.

Railway Village Museum (Faringdon Rd) Restored foreman's house next to the former railway museum, furnished in typical turn-of-the-century working-class style; open mid Apr–Oct; £1 (free with ticket to Steam). Not far from here, the Gluepot (Emlyn Sq) has decent food in a down-to-earth atmosphere.

Swindon & Cricklade Railway (Blunsdon, off B4553 N of Swindon) One of the only-live-steam projects in the area, gradually being restored, with occasional trips through the countryside, and small museum. Snacks, shop, disabled access; cl wkdys, 25–26 Dec; (01793) 771615; around £6.

56. Farm fun for young children

Cholderton Rare Breeds Farm (Amesbury Rd, Cholderton, just off A338) Fun, friendly and well laid out, good for families with young children. There are plenty of opportunities to get close to the animals, inc the youngest of the 60 or so breeds of rabbit they keep. You can also pet pygmy goats and sheep, and other friendly residents include Coco the donkey and Ebenezer the goat. A long-standing favourite with visitors is their National Grunt pig racing (twice a day at wknds and in school hols, usually around 12.30 and 3.30 pm); also tractor and trailer rides, a couple of play areas inc one for under-7s, and new trampolines. Nature trails lace through orchards and woodland, and there are tranquil water gardens in the attractive grounds. Meals, snacks (good cream teas), shop, disabled access; cl Nov–Mar; (01980) 629438; £4.25. The Malet Arms at Newton Tony does good lunches.

57. Friendly farm and picture-book castle

Farmer Giles Farmstead (Teffont Magna) Friendly working dairy farm, with 150 cows milked every afternoon; children can feed some of the animals, or simply sit and stroke them. Also tractor rides, play areas, old farming equipment, and small vineyard. Meals, snacks, shop, disabled access; cl wkdys Nov–Mar;

(01722) 716338; £3.95. The village is very attractive, full of charming stone-built cottages with neatly banked stone-walled gardens; the Black Horse has good food.

Old Wardour Castle (a couple of miles S of Tisbury) Remains of a substantial 14th-c lakeside castle. Though badly damaged in the Civil War, its walls still stand to their original 18 metres (60 ft), and you can walk almost to the top (signs give a good idea what life was like when the castle was still lived in). It's a lovely peaceful setting, landscaped in the 18th c (and used for Kevin Costner's *Robin Hood* in the 20th); there are country walks of varying lengths from the car park. Snacks, shop, disabled access to grounds only; cl 24–26 Dec, 1 Jan; (01747) 870487; £2.50; EH. The lovely old Crown in Tisbury does decent food.

58. Longleat

(off A362 4m W of Warminster) Some stately homes give the impression of opening their doors to the masses rather grudgingly, but this busy estate has thrown itself into the role with gusto. It was one of the first lived-in houses to open to the public, over 50 years ago, and these days it's firmly geared to visitors – but not so much that the attractive grounds have lost any of their appeal. Few places can boast such a range of activities for families; many would merit a visit on their own, and there's easily enough to fill a whole day or even longer (the ticket allows you to spread the attractions over more than one visit). Children will probably get most excited about the safari park, which as well as the famous lions has rhinos, camels, elephants and a rare white tiger; unusually, you can walk through some parts, the fine beech trees and parkland an appealing backdrop to giraffes, llamas and zebras. A bus can take you round if you haven't got your own car, though you'll need to book a place on it fairly quickly. With sea lions swimming beside you, a boat trip leads to Gorilla Island, where two gorillas live in comparative luxury: their miniature stately home has central heating, games and even satellite TV. Vegetables have been planted to encourage them to dig for food as they would in the wild, but with a lifestyle like theirs you wouldn't be surprised if they expected meals delivered on a platter. Among what seem like hundreds of other attractions are displays of parrots and butterflies, a narrow-gauge railway, collection of dolls' houses, and exhibitions based around the rather differing worlds of Postman Pat and Doctor Who (you can make yourself sound like a Dalek). An extraordinarily elaborate play area is set in a full-size mock castle; there are different sections for different age groups (except adults, allowed in only if they bring their own child). There's also a simulator ride and children's petting zoo. Older visitors may prefer the more peaceful formal gardens laid out by Capability Brown; a well liked beauty spot, Heaven's Gate, now has its own rival to Stonehenge – nine massive sculpted standing stones. And of course there's the handsome 16th-c house itself, much restored inside, but with impressively grand formal rooms, and the individual murals of the colourful current Marquis of Bath. He has had several mazes and labyrinths built around the grounds: the yew hedge maze is Britain's longest, taking visitors an average of 90 minutes to find their way out. Another has a slightly saucy shape that can be appreciated only from the Marquis's own private roof terrace, but perhaps the most frustrating is a bewildering knot of mirrors, with animatronic effects adding to the confusion. There's a busy calendar of extra events, and you can get coarse fishing permits. Dogs on a lead are allowed in some areas. Meals, snacks, shop, disabled access; most attractions, inc the safari park, are cl from early Nov to late Mar, but the house is open all year (cl 25 Dec; in winter guided tours only); (01985) 844400. You can get individual tickets for the attractions, but it works out much cheaper to buy the all-in

Passport Ticket, £14 adults, £11 children 4–14. This allows one visit to everything, but you don't have to do it all in one day.

59. Clifftop chairlift, multi-coloured sands, and much more

Needles Park (Alum Bay) Clifftop pleasure park which stands out for its spectacular chairlift down to the beach, with wonderful views along the way; also crazy golf, a new simulator ride, and they sell little glass tubes with differently coloured sands carefully layered inside. Meals, snacks, shop, disabled access; cl early Nov–Easter; (01983) 752401; park entry free (though car parking is £3), then individual charges for attractions (£6.50 for saver ticket covering main attractions). Glass-blowing demonstrations at adjacent Alum Bay Glass, and tours of the Sweet Manufactory (cl over Christmas; 80p each); both have good factory shops.

Needles Old Battery From Needles Park it's a mile walk to this 19th-c Palmerstonian fort (you can't go by car); the parade-ground shows off two 12-ton gun barrels salvaged from the sea, and there's an exhibition about World War I. A 60-metre (200-ft) tunnel leads to a look-out spot that gives stunning views of the Needles themselves, a group of wave-battered chalk pinnacles, and their lighthouse. Good views from their 1940s-style tearoom; cl Fri and Sat (exc July–Aug), all Nov–Mar, and in bad weather; (01983) 754772; £3; NT.

The beach in Alum Bay is famous for its multi-coloured sands from the different rock strata in the cliff that runs down to it; 20 shades of pinks, greys and ochres, showing up most vividly after rain. The High Down Hotel towards Totland has decent food.

60. Dinosaurs, goblins and smugglers

Blackgang Chine Fantasy Park (Blackgang) This 40-acre family leisure park has an excellent policy on return visits: each ticket allows £1 entry for a second visit within four days. The liveliest attraction is an enjoyable high-speed water chute, and there are plenty more gentle rides to suit younger children, inc a badger-themed fairground. The most interesting parts are the maritime museum at the restored quayside, and the complete replica of a Victorian sawmill, inc working steam and oil engines. Lots of models of dinosaurs, goblins, and nursery rhyme scenes dotted around the gardens (pretty on summer evenings when they're illuminated). Also fossils and gemstones, a hedge maze, and several play areas, inc one for toddlers. Meals, snacks, shop, disabled access (some steep hills); open late Mar–Oct; (01983) 730330; £6.50 (children 3–13 £5.50). The Wight Mouse at Chale is an excellent family pub, and the A3055 in both directions gives fine sea and coast views.

Museum of Smuggling History (Ventnor) In the Botanic Garden (or more correctly under it), this demonstrates the tricks smugglers past and present have used to sneak in wool, brandy, tobacco or drugs. Shop; cl Oct–Mar; (01983) 853677; £2.40. The steep Botanic Garden is full of unusual tropical-look plants.

Ventnor is a relatively untouristy little clifftop town, the fairly restrained and decorous seafront down below linked to it by a tortuously steep loop of road; between them perched on ledges among the trees are quite a number of Victorian villas – many of them still private houses rather than guesthouses. The **Heritage Museum** on Spring Hill is good for local history (limited disabled access; cl 12.30–2, Weds and Sat pm, all Sun, and Nov–mid-May; 75p). The Spyglass is an interesting pub with superb sea views, and the seafront Mill Bay is good too.

61. Robin Hill Country Park

(Downend) A very useful retreat for families, particularly those with younger children who want to run around. Like its stablemate

Blackgang Chine, it has a few rather dated-looking representations of trolls and the like, but scores more highly for rides such as the pirate ship, the 400-metre toboggan run (best for older children, £1 extra) and the motion-platform cinema. Boasting good play areas, with underground tunnels and assault course equipment, the park also has a pitch and putt course, look-out tower, wooden maze, and plenty of space for football and basketball. An interactive wildlife area has recently been added. Paths and trails wind through the woodland. Meals, snacks, shop, disabled access but rather hilly in parts; cl Nov–Mar; (01983) 527352; £5.50 if you're over 1.1 metre, £3.50 if under; (good value £1 return ticket allows a second visit within four days). The nearby Hare & Hounds is a useful family dining pub, open all day.

62. Jungle wildlife

Amazon World (Watery Lane, Newchurch; A3056) Among the 200 species is everything from marmosets and crocodiles, through toucans and flamingos, to tarantulas and terrapins. New acquisitions this year include anteaters, tree porcupines and gold lion tamarins. There are some bigger animals outdoors, but as most of the exhibition is under cover, it's enjoyable in any weather. Divided into several areas, it starts with the story of the rain forests, then goes on to look at how man lives and works in them, the damage that's been done to rain forests in recent years, and a look at the campaigns to reverse that. Outside is an area where children can touch and feed rabbits, goats and the like, as well as twice-daily falconry displays (weather permitting) at 12.30 and 3.30pm. They have meet the animal sessions every day at 2pm, where a keeper shows off two animals at a time. There's an adventure playground, with a separate area for under-5s, and a new study centre displaying a dinosaur dig. Meals, snacks, picnic areas, shop, disabled access; cl 25–26 Dec, the first week in Jan; (01983) 867122; £5.25 (£4 children 3–14).

The White Lion in nearby Arreton does good value lunches.

63. Make friends with exotic birds and animals

Flamingo Park Wildlife Encounter (B3330, Seaview) Attractively laid out in spacious landscaped grounds, this friendly and nicely unspoilt place has far more than just the flamingos from whom it takes its name. There are all sorts of other tame exotic birds, and what makes it really special is the way you can get so close to them; many will feed from your hand, and it's quite a thrill seeing them swoop down towards you. The talks by keepers are great for children: they try to bring out the birds' individual characteristics, as well as passing on a conservation message. Events and demonstrations throughout the day include feeding penguins, pelicans, macaws and parrots; there's also a new display of brightly coloured free-flying exotic birds, owls, and some delightful baby penguins splashing around in their nursery pool. They have other animals too, notably beavers and red squirrels, with hands-on opportunities at the recently extended pets corner. You can also usually feed their koi and huge mirror carp. It's all arranged with some thought and style, but hasn't been over-developed, and they take care to ensure everyone who wants to will feed a bird at some stage of their visit. No dogs. Meals, snacks, shop, picnic areas, disabled access; cl Nov–Mar; (01983) 612153; £5.25 adults, £3.50 children. A family ticket (two adults, two children) is £16.

In Seaview, lunch at the Seaview Hotel (High St) is quite a treat.

64. A great day out for younger kids

Paultons Park (Ower) Agreeable family leisure park with over 40 attractions and rides, gardens, animals, birds and wildfowl, as well as model dinosaurs in marshland, a ten-acre lake with working waterwheel, hedge maze, animated scenes from *The Wind in the Willows*, and unique Romany Experience with the sights, sounds and smells of traditional gypsy life. The new swingboat and roundabout rides join attractions such as the Raging River log flume, tea-cups, go-karts (the only thing with an extra charge), bumper boats, roller-coaster and several good play areas, many ideal for toddlers. Meals, snacks, shop, disabled access; cl wkdys Nov and Dec (exc Christmas specials), and all Jan–mid-Mar; (023) 8081 4455; £10.50, various family tickets available.

The Rockingham Arms at Canada, off the A36 Romsey rd not far from here, does enjoyable family food, and has the New Forest practically on its doorstep.

65. Beaulieu Abbey

Rated a great day out by readers, its centrepiece is the National Motor Museum, a collection that from humble beginnings has become one of the most comprehensive in the world. Other features have a motoring theme too: a hands-on gallery explains how cars work, and Wheels is probably the highlight for children – you sit in a pod-like vehicle and trundle through 100 years of motoring. For an extra £2 a simulator ride gives you a more robust driving experience. A monorail whizzes round the grounds, and in summer you can ride on a replica 1912 London bus. Also go-kart style mini-bikes, radio-controlled cars, and some hi-tech arcade-style driving games. Meanwhile the Palace House is a fine old mansion based around the gatehouse of the huge Cistercian Abbey that stood here until the Reformation (still with what are thought to be the original monastic fan-vaulted ceilings). The surrounding lakeside parkland and gardens are rewarding to explore, with ruins of other abbey buildings, and an exhibition on the monks who lived here. Meals, snacks, shops, disabled access; cl 25 Dec; (01590) 612345; £9.95.

In the village facing the Palace House gates, Montys is popular for lunch, and a pleasant 2½ mile riverside walk leads from here down to the very pretty little waterside village of Bucklers Hard, where long red-roofed cottage rows flank a wide, grassed waterside street. It was once an important centre for shipbuilding, and the Maritime Museum tells the story of the industry, right up to the voyages of Sir Francis Chichester. You have to pay to come into the village, though admission includes entry to the museum and the various other exhibitions and reconstructions dotted around, inc the carefully restored 18th-c homes of a shipwright and labourer, and a typical inn scene complete with costumed figures, smells and conversation. Snacks, shop; cl 25 Dec; (01590) 616203; £3.50. There are summer boat trips, and the Master Builders House is useful for lunch.

66. Big guns and secret tunnels

Fort Nelson (Downend Rd, Fareham) You don't have to be interested in weaponry to enjoy a trip to this restored 19th-c fort, built in response to fears of an attack from France, and now part of the Royal Armouries Museum. It has been known as the noisiest museum in the world, thanks mainly to the roar of the two huge cannons fired twice a day, usually at 12 and 3pm, and the lingering smell of gunpowder adds to the atmosphere. Children aren't discouraged from clambering over the building and even some of the exhibits (which go back well beyond guns – they've recently acquired the catapult used in the film *Gladiator*). With plenty of underground tunnels to investigate, it's not unlike an enormous adventure playground. Occasional battle re-enactment days (best to ring for dates), and regular guided tours. Good views of Portsmouth Harbour from the ramparts. Meals, snacks, shop, disabled access; cl 25 Dec; (01329) 233734; £4.25, children free. The Osborne View (Hill Head) has popular food and superb views, and is handy for the beach and walks in Titchfield Haven nature reserve.

67. Explosion!

(Priddy's Hard, Priory Rd, Gosport) Yes, that's its name, and very apt. Small boys of all ages will be particularly excited by this splendid new museum of naval firepower, but it has a much wider appeal than that; the often lively displays offer a fascinating look at not just how weaponry has been made and used over the years, but also the effect it has on those who produce it (for example workers making TNT found their hair went red) – not to mention the people on the receiving end. The 18th-c naval stores it's housed in are fairly extensive, and there's plenty to see, from old muskets to the latest Exocet missiles. There are rooms devoted to small arms, mines, big guns, submarines and torpedoes; most have some kind of interactive feature or touch screen displays (from quizzes to explanations of how a rifle works), and children are able to handle lots of the hardware – it's not at all the kind of place where you're discouraged from touching things. A highlight is the well laid out and atmospheric Grand Magazine, where a number of films put the building and its history nicely in context, with enough booms and bangs to satisfy most tastes. Children's favourite bits include a section with a moving floor and video, to show how hard it was to load guns while on a moving deck at sea (it really is disorienting, but you can stop it with a button before you get seasick), and a challenge to see how many wooden bullets you can load into a gun in a minute (the record so far is around 45).

They've taken pains to make it relevant to girls as well, with displays on the lives of female munitions workers. Don't worry if it all sounds rather militaristic – it doesn't glorify weapons or wars at all. You'll need at least a couple of hours to get round. There may be extra activities in school holidays. It's part of an extensive scheme to rejuvenate Portsmouth Harbour, and by far the best way to get there in fine weather is to take the three-minute ferry from Portsmouth, and stroll along the new Millennium Promenade. Waterside meals and snacks, shop, disabled access; cl 25–26 Dec, 1 Jan; (023) 9250 5600; £5 adults, £3 children. A family ticket for two adults and up to four children is very good value at £13; one adult and three children is £11.

A good spot for lunch is the Alverbank House Hotel (Stokes Bay Rd), in woods at the end of Walpole Park, over the rd from the Alverstoke promenade; it's got a nice big garden with a play area.

68. Our greatest fighting ships

HM Naval Base is the main stop for most visitors to Portsmouth, with lots to see. It houses **HMS *Victory***, the ***Mary Rose***, **HMS *Warrior***, and the **Royal Naval Museum**. The flagship is of course **HMS *Victory***, still in commission, and manned by regular serving officers. Guided tours bring those Trafalgar days very close, and include the spot where Nelson died. The raising of the ***Mary Rose*** from the Solent silt where it had sat for 437 years provided a wealth of material and information about the Tudor period. The discoveries are well shown in an airy hall, while the great oak hull itself is in a separate shed, sprayed almost constantly to prevent the timbers from drying out (there are plans to build a new ship hall as part of the harbour redevelopment). **HMS *Warrior*** when launched 140 years ago was the most fearsome battleship in the world; she's been immaculately restored, and is manned by tars in period uniform. Again, tours are very vivid. Action Stations gives a new look at the modern navy through an IMAX film and interactive displays. Housed in handsome 18th-c dockside buildings, the **Royal Naval Museum** has lively displays on the development and history of the navy up to and beyond the Falklands War (or as it's called here the South Atlantic Campaign), with interactive galleries looking at Nelson, the sailing navy, and HMS *Victory* (and its role in the Battle of Trafalgar). Lots of Nelson memorabilia, and a very jolly gallery looking at popular images of the sailor. Each ship costs £6.75 to visit individually (though the HMS *Victory* ticket also includes entry to the museum, which on its own costs £3.50). You can also buy a passport ticket (ferry fare included) which covers all the attractions above for £17.50 for a day, or you can choose three attractions for £13.25. The site – which itself costs nothing to enter, after a security check – has a restaurant and shop, and there's disabled access to all the ships; cl 25 Dec; (023) 9272 7562.

The Still & West and Spice Island family pubs have great harbourside positions, with plenty to watch on the water.

69. Fishes and Commandos

Portsmouth Aquarium (Clarence Esplanade, Southsea) Excellent for families, with all sorts of multi-sensory experiences and displays, and an exciting shark encounter. Children complete a scratchcard trail as they go round, and there's an indoor soft play area. Snacks, shop, disabled access; cl Nov–Feb for refurbishment; (023) 9287 5222; £5.25 (they'll stamp your hand and let you come back later in the day). There are boat trips round the harbour from nearby.

Royal Marines Museum (Eastney Esplanade, Southsea) This vigorous place couldn't be more different from the usual military exhibitions – lively re-creations of major amphibious actions, a junior commando assault course, and a jungle room with a real snake and scorpion. Also lots of changing exhibitions and special events. Snacks, shop, disabled access; cl three days over Christmas; (023) 9281 9385; *£4.

The Tenth Hole (Eastern Parade) is a good bustling café overlooking the seafront pitch-and-putt course, but doesn't allow under-12s.

70. A bargain day out around Portsmouth

Southsea Castle The fortifications in defence of Portsmouth Harbour, here, around Gosport, and up on Portsdown, give a remarkably complete picture of the development of defensive strategy from Tudor times to the fears of French invasion in the 1860s, though they have more appeal to people interested in warfare than to those who like the romantic idea of a regular 'castle'. Southsea Castle and Museum is the best place to start, built in 1545 as part of Henry VIII's coastal defences. Good displays on Portsmouth's military history, and a time-tunnel experience of the history of the castle; special events (esp summer). Shop; cl Nov–Mar; (023) 9282 7261; £2.50.

City Museum (Museum Rd) Very good displays on the city's history, in an astonishing former barracks that looks rather like a French château. Also decorative art and crafts. Snacks, shop, disabled access; cl 25–26 Dec; (023) 9282 7261; free.

Queen Elizabeth Country Park (Gravel Hill, NE of Clanfield) Lots going on all year, with woodland walks and rides (stables at the park), open downland, an adventure play trail, and events such as Easter egg rolling. You can arrange horse riding; (023) 9259 9669. Disabled access; park open all year, visitor centre, shop and café cl wkdys Jan–Mar; (023) 9259 5040; £1.50 parking charge Sun and bank hols, £1 rest of wk. In fine weather a picnic would be the best thing here; otherwise, the Five Bells not far off at Buriton has a good choice of popular food.

71. Fun at the farm, and Iron Age life

Finkley Down Farm Park (just NE of Andover) Well laid out working farm with wide range of animals and poultry inc rare breeds; they encourage you to touch the tamer animals, and there are varied activities every half-hour. Also countryside museum, adventure playground and picnic site. Readers rate this very highly, and it has lots for children (inc space for them to run around). Meals, snacks, shop, disabled access; cl Nov–Feb; (01264) 352195; £4.25

   Museum of the Iron Age (Andover) Nr the church at the top of the impressive High St of this very extended country town, the museum looks particularly at finds from nearby Danebury Ring, giving a vivid impression of life for the pre-Roman Celts. Snacks, shop, limited disabled access; cl Sun–Mon, and Christmas; (01264) 366283; free. There's an adjacent more general **museum** (open same hours, free).

   There are well stocked trout fishing lakes around Andover, inc Rooksbury Mill. Poplar Farm (A343 at Abbotts Ann) is a useful food stop.

72. Hampshire life and crafts, past and present

Milestones Living History Museum (Leisure Park, off B3400, Churchill Way W, Basingstoke) A network of streets and authentically assembled buildings has been constructed to re-create the sights, sounds and smells of local life since Victorian times, with factories, a railway station, brewery (an attached pub will serve ales from Hampshire brewer Gales), fire station, and shops. Period lampposts have been moved here from Winchester, and they've dotted around freeze-dried mice and stuffed pigeons. Staff in period clothes will explain things; the whole thing is indoors, in a splendid very modern-looking glass building. The idea is to showcase dozens of previously undisplayed collections and items, and there's an interactive post office for under-5s, where children will be able to sort and stamp letters for posting throughout the museum, a big toy area where activity trucks compare today's toys and games with those from the past, and a hands-on history section for 7- to 11-year-olds, with a fun old-fashioned photographer's studio (you can have your picture taken on some wknds). There is some emphasis on local industries, with vehicles and collections relating to Thornycroft, Willis and Stevens, steam engines from Taskers of Andover, and early examples of clothing from Burberrys, whose first shop opened in Basingstoke in 1856. Good value meals and snacks, shop, disabled access; cl 24–26, 31 Dec, and 1 Jan; (01256) 477766; £5.95 (£2.95 children). The surrounding leisure park has ice-skating, cinemas and ten-pin bowling.

Viables Craft Centre (Harrow Way, off A30 and via Grove Rd off A339, Basingstoke) Fourteen craft workshops in and around an 18th-c timber granary; ceramics studio, art and craft gallery, miniature railway, model car racing circuit, and various courses all year. Meals, snacks, disabled access; usually only cl Sun but best to check; (01256) 473634; free.

Though it's out past the other side of Basingstoke, the Gamekeepers in the pretty village of Mapledurwell is a good dining pub, with lots of pleasant footpaths nearby.

73. Birdworld & Underwater World

(Holt Pound, off A325 3m SW of Farnham – actually just over the Hampshire border) Very attractive to wander round, this popular place has masses of birds spread over 26 acres of thoughtfully laid out gardens and parkland; it's a nice alternative to the county's two big theme parks. Species here take in all shapes and sizes, from tiny tanagers to rheas, emus and ostriches. Children can go right up to some of the birds, and to the animals in the farmyard (some of which they can feed); there's always a section with baby birds which delights younger ones. They have a good programme of shows, feeding sessions and displays; each day's events are listed on a sheet you'll be given as you go in. The twice-daily penguin feeding is always a favourite: you can arrange in advance for your child to do the feeding. Other highlights include the parrots flying around their aviary, and the decent aquarium, **Underwater World**, with tropical and other freshwater and marine fish, and a few alligators in a jungly swamp. There are several good play areas, and regular children's activities in the school holidays. They have interesting talks on their birds of prey, though the feeding of these is not for the squeamish: some eat dead chicks. Plenty of shelters if it rains, and as many features are under cover it's still a decent bet when the weather looks iffy. The woodland trail leads round to a very good, extensive garden centre. The whole site can get quite busy in summer. Meals, snacks, shop, disabled access; usually cl wkdys Nov–mid-Feb (exc Christmas hols); (01420) 22140; £8.50 adults, £5.50 children 3–14. A family ticket (two adults, two children) is £24.95, and you can save 10% off all prices by booking in advance on-line at www.birdworld.co.uk (provided it's more than two days before your visit). The nearby 16th-c Cherry Tree at Rowledge has good food.

74. Balloons, bridge-building and boating

Guildford Discovery Science Centre (Ward St) Primarily for children but enjoyed by adults too, this thoroughly hands-on centre (all the exhibits are designed to be handled) is a lively but thorough introduction to the mysteries of science. The range of activities includes the chance to build your own suspension bridge or send a hot-air balloon to the ceiling, and they have a good programme of events inc science shows and experiments (especially in the school hols). Shop, disabled access with notice; cl Sun am and all Mon; may be moving to Weybridge after Christmas 2001, so best to ring before you set off; 01483 537080; £2.75.

Guildford Boat House (Millbrook) Old-established boat house where you can hire boats for the Wey Navigation; from £6 an hour; (01483) 504494. Nearby the newly refurbished Jolly Farmer does decent food in a lovely riverside setting.

75. Chessington World of Adventures

(A243) Excellently put together, this is the place to head for unadulterated fun. The big thrill ride is Rameses' Revenge, which spins you round 360 degrees at speeds of up to 60 mph, while plummeting towards a rock-lined pit where you'll be sprayed by water jets. The hanging roller-coaster the Vampire (closed for refurbishment, but due to reopen in spring), is equally traumatic, and though the more traditional-seeming Rattlesnake looks a little gentler it still packs quite a punch (all have height restrictions). There's plenty to amuse younger children, from the Dragon River log flume and Action Man Training HQ to the simpler rides around Toytown. They'll also get the most out of the once-famous zoo from which everything else developed; over on the quieter, greener side of the park, it's now rather lost among the other attractions, but there are sea lion and penguin displays at set times throughout the day, and a good reptile and insect house. A monorail gives bird's-eye views of the lions, tigers and meerkats, and now from an African-style game lodge you can watch their large family of gorillas. Meals, snacks, shop, some disabled access but best to phone in advance; open Apr–Oct (exc some days towards the end of the season, so phone to check); (0870) 4447777; full-priced entry is rather expensive, at £19.95, but if you get here early enough and spend the whole day you won't feel cheated. The Star down towards the M25 is a good value food stop.

76. An A24 day mixing wine-making with a friendly farm

Denbies Wine Estate (A24 just N of Dorking) Britain's biggest vineyard, and at 265 acres bigger than most in Europe. The tour is unique and you don't have to be a wine buff to enjoy it. Beginning with a 20-minute film in their unusual 360-degree cinema, you are then taken through the winery on a road train to the cellars where you can try out some of their produce. A new train tour takes you round the vineyard (Apr–Oct, £4). Meals and snacks (in unusually designed restaurant), big shop, good disabled access; cl 25 Dec, 1 Jan; (01306) 876616; £7.25, combined ticket for outdoor and indoor tours £10.25. Fine views and walks nearby.

The 16th-c Kings Arms in Dorking's West St has decent food.

Box Hill nearby is Surrey's most popular viewpoint, with a summit car park and walks on its steep juniper and boxwood slopes: wild orchids and butterflies in early summer, maybe field mushrooms in early autumn. It's a good place for picnics – or the attractively placed King William IV at Mickleham is excellent for lunch.

Horton Park Children's Farm (B280 W of Epsom) Plenty of animals to feed and cuddle, tractor rides (a little extra), an adventure playground and indoor play area. Meals, snacks and picnic area, shop, disabled access; cl 25–26 Dec; (01372) 743984; £3.90 each child (one accompanying adult free).

77. Ancient crafts revived in reconstructed village

Weald & Downland Open-Air Museum (A286, Singleton) Fascinating collection of over 40 historic buildings rescued from all over the South-East, dismantled and re-erected here. They're arranged to form an authentic-looking village, with outlying farm and agricultural buildings, medieval farmstead and shops, blacksmith's forge, tollhouse and Victorian schoolroom. You can buy flour from the working watermill, and when it's completed, you'll be able to watch experts restore timber frames in a timber-built but futuristic new gridshell building. Well organised children's activities might include brick-laying or basket-making. Snacks, shop, some disabled access, but the site is rather steep; open daily Mar–Oct, then Weds and wknds Nov–Feb, plus Christmas wk; (01243) 811348; £7. The 16th-c Fox & Hounds nearby is a good stop.

78. Historic cars, exotic waterfowl and lots of action

Bentley Wildfowl & Motor Museum (Halland) Busy estate centred around Tudor farmhouse converted into Palladian mansion, filled with fine furnishings and paintings, inc watercolours by local artist Phillip Rickman. The motor museum has gleaming veteran, Edwardian and vintage vehicles, while the lakes and ponds that surround it are home to countless varieties of rare and exotic wildfowl. There are also woodland trails, a good adventure playground, on-site craftsmen and artists, and miniature trains that steam through the grounds (wknds Easter–Oct plus Weds in Aug). Special events (no extra price) run from veteran and vintage car and other transport rallies to woodcraft, fire brigade and birds of prey displays. Snacks, shop, disabled access; open daily mid-Mar–Oct (house cl Mar and am), and all exc house also open wknds in Nov, Feb and early Mar; (01825) 840573; £5, less winter.

The Black Lion (A22/B2192) has decent food.

79. A lively adventure park

Knockhatch (A22, W of Hailsham) Plenty to do in this 80-acre park which has a birds of prey centre, hands-on farm and adventure playgrounds as well as more unusual attractions like a laser adventure game (£3.25), and karting (£3.50). Also crazy golf, boating lake, woodland trail and picnic area. Snacks, shop, disabled access; open wknds and school hols Feb–Oct; (01323) 442051; £5.75.

80. A great zoo for children

Drusillas Park (Alfriston, up towards A27) They keep only animals that they can provide with everything they'd have in the wild, so no lions, tigers or elephants, but plenty of smaller and arguably more entertaining creatures; it's certainly a great hit with children. You watch the meerkats through a little dome, there's a walk-through fruit bat enclosure, and Penguin Bay has underwater viewpoints. Elsewhere is everything from snakes and other creepy-crawlies to a splendid range of monkeys. There's a farmyard area, and Pet World gives younger visitors a chance to get closer to rabbits and guinea-pigs (who now have a new village), chinchillas and maybe even snakes. The play areas are excellent, a jolly little railway chuffs its way around the park, and they've recently added a jungle-themed miniature golf course. Some of the extras have an additional charge: an activity centre open at wknds and in school holidays costs 50p for mask-making, £2.60 for face-painting, and £1 to pan for gold. Good meals and snacks, picnic areas, shops, excellent disabled access; cl 24–26 Dec; (01323) 874100; £7.99.

Alfriston is one of the South-East's showcase villages – at quieter times of the year (in high summer the ice-cream eaters, teashops and curio shops somewhat blunt its appeal). It has thatched, tiled and timbered houses, and a fine church built on a Saxon funeral barrow, by a large green just off the single main st. One of the most engaging buildings in the village is the Star Inn, with its Old Bill, a bright red figurehead lion on one corner taken as a trophy from a 17th-c Dutch ship, and some intricate painted 15th-c carvings among its handsome timbering – it's fun trying to work out what they could all mean. The ancient George opposite it, simpling oozing age, is good for lunch. Just over a mile S of the village, the road gives good views of the famous Cuckmere meanders, as the river winds intricately through the valley.

81. Seven Sisters Sheep Centre

(Gilberts Drive, East Dean) A particularly enjoyable and genuine place to visit, this unspoilt family-run downland sheep farm remains especially good value for families hoping to see a proper working farm. With 47 different species, they have the biggest collection of sheep breeds anywhere in the world, some tame enough to touch and feed. The best time to come is the lambing season between March and May, when children can bottle feed the lambs, but there's plenty going on when they reopen later in the summer, with daily shearing and wool handling displays. There's a good commentary when the sheep are milked, and demonstrations of yoghurt- and cheese-making. Other animals include pigs, horses, goats, chickens and ducks, with a new barn where children can fuss rabbits, chinchillas and so on. Younger visitors also enjoy the tractor/trailer ride across the farm (50p extra). The farm shop sells cheese and other products made from ewe's milk. Snacks, good disabled access (paved paths between the pens); open 2 Mar–5 May, then 6 July–8 Sept, usually cl am wkdys (exc bank hols) but best to check; (01323) 423302; *£3.25 adults, £2.25 children 2–15. A family ticket (two adults and two children) is £10 – not bad for a couple of hours' honest and informative entertainment.

The village itself is prettily set around a sloping green, with an attractive pub, the Tiger. A lane past the farm continues to the Birling Gap, a cleft in the coastal cliffs famous since smuggling days, with walks up to Belle Tout, a former coastguard station and lighthouse moved back 17 metres (55 ft) in 1999 to save it from coastal erosion; the path continues to Beachy Head.

82. A day out in Eastbourne

Museum of Shops (Cornfield Terr) One of the most comprehensive collections of its type, 20 reconstructed and very well filled shops and rooms, inc an old seafarers' tavern. Shop, disabled access to ground floor only; cl 24–26 Dec; (01323) 737143; £3.

Redoubt Fortress (Royal Parade) A splendid Napoleonic fort, housing a more interesting than average military museum. Open-air concerts (every Weds and Fri late Jun–early Sept) always end in a firework display. Shop; cl early Nov–Easter; (01323) 410300; £1.50.

Wish Tower (King Edward's Parade) One of the 103 Martello Towers built in case of French invasion; there's a fascinating collection of puppets, some centuries old. Shop; usually open wknds Easter–Oct, plus wkdys mid-July–Aug; (01323) 411620; £1.80.

The Duke of Devonshire still owns much of this civilised and restrained seaside resort; as he prohibits seaside tat the place has a more dignified and solid feel than many of its livelier rivals – it's perfect for gentle seafront strolling, and a promenade links the smart marina with the beach. The church in the Old Town is lavish; next to it the Lamb is a nice old pub.

83. Perfect picture-book castle

Bodiam Castle (Bodiam) A classic example of 14th-c fortification at its peak, with massive walls rising sheer and virtually complete from the romantic moat, and round drum towers steadfastly guarding each corner. Built to withstand attack from the French, it was only ever besieged by other Englishmen, and on both occasions was rather weedily handed over without a fight. The interior was destroyed around the Civil War, and repairs weren't fully completed until Lord Curzon bought it in 1916; he left the castle to the NT in 1925. Plenty of space for picnics, and several enjoyable special events. It's worth reading the leaflet they give you at the car park – most people fail to spot that the lavatories are at this end rather than at the castle itself. Meals, snacks, shop, limited disabled access; cl wkdys Nov to mid-Feb; (01580) 830436; £1.50 for parking, then £3.70 for castle; NT. The Salehurst Halt at Salehurst just W does good lunches. Kent & East Sussex Railway steam trains now run from the Tenterden terminus over the Kent border all the way to Bodiam's restored station. A joint ticket for the railway and the castle is £10 (available from Tenterden). In summer you can link the train with a 45-min boat trip to the castle through peaceful countryside from Newenden (they don't run in bad weather); (01797) 280363 for times; £6.50 return.

Those children fascinated by bonsai trees will want to know that nearby Bodiam Bonsai grow, show and sell these intricate miniatures – but for the peace of your pocket you may want to keep this a secret.

84. Romans and Normans, snakes and owls

Eagle Heights (Eynsford) Readers enjoy this informative birds of prey centre, good in any weather as many displays are indoors (outdoor ones at 12 and 3.30). There's a new reptile house with some incredibly large pythons. You can handle snakes and reptiles (1.45) and meet the owls (2.15pm). Snacks, shop, disabled access; cl wkdys Nov–Feb; (01322) 866466; £5.50.

Eynsford Castle Norman knight's fortress with impressive 9-metre (30-ft) walls, and remains of the hall and ditch; free. There are organised trails from the nearby countryside centre along the River Darent and into woods above the golf course. The Malt Shovel has good seafood.

Lullingstone Roman Villa (just SE off A225) Remains of rather well-to-do 1st- and 2nd-c family's villa, with exceptionally well preserved floor mosaics and an extensive bath complex. Also an early Christian chapel – the only one so far found in a private house. Snacks, shop, limited disabled access; cl 24–26 Dec and 1 Jan; (01322) 863467; *£2.60.

The Malt Shovel (Station Rd) is a good roomy dining pub.

85. Our Naval heritage

Historic Dockyard (Chatham) Excellent 80-acre working museum in the most complete Georgian dockyard in the world – a visit here can easily fill most of the day. Lots to see and do: the Wooden Walls exhibition uses sights, sounds and smells to show how 18th-c warships such as HMS *Victory* were built here. Guided tours have just started of the newly restored 1944 destroyer HMS *Cavalier* (over 50 of her veterans have been involved in the restoration project). You can also look around the Cold War submarine *Ocelot* and watch the restoration of the Victorian sloop *Gannet*. There's an exhibition on the RNLI, with 16 lifeboats. An exhibition centre in the Flagship Brewery (Building 64) even explores the role of beer in the navy (disabled access; open most wkdys; free), and a new gallery charts Chatham's historic relationship with the navy. Also restorations, rope-making demonstrations, craft workshops, and lively events. Meals, snacks, shop, disabled access; open daily Apr–Oct, plus wknds and Weds in Nov, Feb and Mar; (01634) 823800; £8.50. You can get a ticket that includes **boat trips** on the paddle steamer *Kingswear Castle*.

Fort Amherst (Dock Rd) Perhaps the finest surviving 18th-c fort in the country, with massive ditches, gun emplacements, a warren of tunnels and a firing gun battery; 18 acres of parkland. Meals, snacks, shop; cl 25–26 Dec, 1 Jan; (01634) 847747; £4.50. The Command House below by the water does limited but decent food.

86. Hop Farm Country Park

(off A228, Beltring) The distinctive Victorian oast houses used for drying hops are a peculiar charm of Kent and East Sussex; this is the largest surviving group, now converted into a popular and very well organised family outing, with as much for adults as there is for young children. A couple of the galleried barns have comprehensive exhibitions, one on the hop industry, bringing to life with sounds and smells the experience of working on a hop farm, and the other an entertaining social history collection, spread over three floors. Meanwhile another barn has a big three-storey undercover play area. Their farm has more animals than you'll find in quite a few farm parks, as well as the obligatory pets corner, and feeding sessions throughout the day. More unusually, they also have an impressive collection of shire horses; there are stables tours and dray rides – very evocative on a sunny day. Other areas include an exhibition on water, livened up considerably over the last year, with lots of interactive bits added, a collection of tanks and other military vehicles (they're dramatically put through their paces on one July wknd), and a working potter – you can have a go at making and painting your own creation (50p extra). It's the kind of unhurried place where it's nice just to potter: an outdoor adventure playground, paddling pools, sandpits and a bouncy castle ensure younger children won't get bored. Though it's at its best in dry weather, there's enough indoors to merit a visit at other times too (it's a good bet during the winter). Special events most summer wknds. Meals, snacks, picnic areas, some disabled access (not into oast houses); cl 25–26 Dec; (01622) 872068; £6.50 adults, £4.50 children over 4. A family ticket (two adults, two children) is £20.

The friendly Chequers at nearby Laddingford does good food, with plenty for children (and riverside walks within easy reach).

87. Rare farm animals

South of England Rare Breeds Centre (B2067, Woodchurch) Particularly well organised, good value and a great favourite with readers, this 90-acre working farm has one of the largest collections of rare farm animals in Europe, and a Georgian farmstead has recently been rebuilt here after making way for a new railway. Younger visitors may be able to cuddle baby pigs, meet the goats or get close to the residents in the children's barn. It's amazing seeing the different varieties of one species: rabbits here range from the Netherlands Dwarf (around 2 lb) to the British Giant (a heftier 30 lb). Under-5s are well catered for, with paddling pool and sandpit, and there's a good playground for older children nr a picnic area. Lots of walks and trails, and some fine views of the Kentish countryside. Also trailer and tractor rides. Disabled access is particularly good (they do a lot of work with people with physical or learning disabilities). No dogs. Meals, snacks, shop, plant centre; cl 24–26 Dec and every Mon Oct–Mar; (01233) 861493; £3.50.

In the nearby attractive small town of Tenterden, the Eight Bells,

White Lion, William Caxton and Woolpack are all popular for food.

88. Port Lympne Wild Animal Park

(Lympne) In wonderful ornamental parkland around a well restored house, Port Lympne and its sister park Howletts are well known for their genuinely dedicated approach to looking after the rare or endangered animals in their care; animals are kept in enclosures as alike to their natural habitat as possible, with an aim to return them to the wild if they can. They believe the bonds developed between keepers and animals well worth even the rare casualties. There's a lot to see, paths can be steep, and there are 300 acres altogether – the free shuttle trailers between enclosures are welcome. A new family gorilla enclosure is extending the breeding programme (shared with Howletts) of 65 lowland gorillas, the most successful of its kind in the world. The park is also home to the country's largest breeding herd of black rhino. Other animals include tigers, elephants, lions and tapirs, and they hold occasional special talks and events. The house has unusual features, inc the Hexagonal Library used to sign the Treaty of Paris after World War I, Rex Whistler's incredible Tent Room, and one room entirely covered by a mural showing south-east Asian animals and birds. Meals, snacks, shop; cl 25 Dec; (01303) 264646; £9.80.

89. Dover Castle

Not to be missed, an excellently preserved magnificent Norman fortress with its original keep, 74-metre (242-ft) well and massive walls and towers. There's a lot to see inc the atmospheric complex of underground tunnels that played a vital role in World War II, and an exhibition which dramatically re-creates an early 13th-c siege. Also included are the Pharos Tower, a Roman lighthouse using a 4th-floor flaring brazier as a guide-light, and a restored Saxon church. A walk round the battlements gives interesting views of the comings and goings down in the harbour (something which captivates small children); you can get an audioguide to listen to as you stroll. Snacks, shop, disabled access; cl 24–26 Dec, 1 Jan; (01304) 211067; £7 (£3.50 children), family ticket (two adults and up to three children) £17.50; EH.

Blakes (Castle St) is useful for lunch.

90. Howletts Zoo

(signed off A2; Bekesbourne) The first of the excellent wildlife parks founded by the late John Aspinall. Well spread over lovely grounds, it's well known (along with its bigger sister park at Lympne, see entry 88) for its genuinely dedicated approach to looking after the rare or endangered animals and – more controversially, because of the danger – the bonds developed between the keepers and the animals. Highlights include the world's largest colony of breeding gorillas (over 100 have been born here, and two have been successfully released into the wild), and a unique herd of breeding elephants. Other animals include deer, antelope, leopards and gibbons. Meals, snacks, shop, disabled access; cl 25 Dec; (01227) 721286; £9.80.

In nearby Bekesbourne Hill, the Unicorn has good home-made food, and in Bridge, we can recommend the food at the Red Lion and the White Horse.

91. London

For London, instead of putting together standardised days out, we give notes on some of its most enjoyable places, so that you can pick and choose, either for just one highlight of a day visit, or taking in several for an exhaustingly action-packed day. Of course, for children who haven't seen them before, it's almost essential to have a look at Buckingham Palace (the Guard changes at 11.30, but only every second day in winter), Trafalgar Square, the Houses of Parliament with Big Ben, the River Thames (with perhaps a boat trip from Embankment or Westminster piers), and Piccadilly Circus (nearby in the Trocadero, Funland is an indoor theme park with some excellent rides and state-of-the-art arcade games).

St James's Park The oldest of London's Royal Parks, it was drained and converted into a deer park for Henry VIII, redesigned in the style of Versailles by order of Charles II (who often went for walks through it), and then reworked by Nash for George IV – this is the park which we see today, its relaxing lakeside environment particularly enjoyed by lunch-breaking office workers (and by hundreds of more or less exotic waterfowl), with a brass band in summer. It's beautifully floodlit at night, and on Sun traffic is barred from its roads. It makes a splendid link between Buckingham Palace at one end and either Parliament Sq or (through the Admiralty Arch) Trafalgar Sq at the other, and half way down are the elegant brick buildings of St James's Palace – Old London at its best.

Covent Garden Partly pedestrianised, the former vegetable, fruit and flower market with its elegant buildings is now made over to smart café-bars, boutiques and stalls, such as those in the covered piazza, selling good but expensive handmade clothes and craft items. There's a bustling cosmopolitan atmosphere, and good street entertainers, and it's always fun to wander around. The streets around are full of unusual shops: Knutz (Russell St) has everything for the practical joker, for instance. The Africa Centre on King St may have exhibitions of African art and culture. No shortage of places to eat around here.

London Transport Museum (The Piazza, Covent Garden)

On the site of the former Flower Market, this is a surprisingly fun attraction. You can race a tram and a bus, delve into feely boxes, design your own bus and see why a steam train doesn't suit the Underground. The main show is quite traditional, but they don't mind if you climb aboard some of the buses, trams and tube trains, and the touch screens throughout are much more enticing for children than traditional information boards. Costumed actors tell nostalgic transport tales, and there might be story-telling, face-painting or craft workshops in school hols. Snacks, interesting shop, disabled access; usually cl 24–26 Dec but best to check over Christmas; (020) 7836 8557; £5.95.

Theatre Museum (Russell St, Covent Garden) Exhaustive look at events and personalities on the stage over the last few hundred years. Posters, puppets and props are among the permanent collection, which although astonishingly comprehensive is arranged a little confusingly; it's easy to find yourself going round backwards. The very good temporary displays leave the deepest impression: there are always free stage make-up demonstrations and you can dress up at the costume workshops. Shop, disabled access; cl Mon and bank hols; (020) 7943 4700; free.

Natural History Museum (Cromwell Rd, South Kensington) One of the most appealing places for families in the capital, constantly updating or adding attractions, and with displays that could keep most visitors enthralled for a week. Picking out highlights of this wonderful place isn't easy, but younger visitors still most enjoy the parts you'd expect – in particular the dinosaurs. There's a whole gallery devoted to the fearsome beasts, with lots of touch-screen activities and information. More gently evocative are the complete skeletons in the museum's main hall, a grand and noble sight below the intricately painted ceilings of the remarkable Romanesque building. The creepy-crawlies are another good bet: you can get a taste on their website (www.nhm.ac.uk), which every few seconds displays fresh images from their ant colony. The Earth Galleries are worth putting near the top of your list; there's an earthquake simulator, and you can see where real earthquakes have occurred in the last few days. Remember to pick up one of the maps and guides as you go in, as it's a vast place, covering four acres. Meals, snacks, shops (one is dinosaur-themed), disabled access; cl 25–26 Dec; 020 7942 5000; free.

Science Museum (Exhibition Rd, South Kensington) Amazing museum, with its splendid Wellcome Wing devoted entirely to contemporary science, medicine and technology. Other galleries look at subjects such as genetics, the internet and the future role of science; there's also an IMAX cinema (£6.75). The area has been designed to hold fast-changing, interactive exhibitions with plenty of hands-on displays, workshops and demonstrations, and a multi-sensory activity area aimed at under-8s (but parents seem to love it too). Elsewhere in the museum, exhibits range from Stephenson's *Rocket* to the Apollo 10 space capsule, and there are newly landscaped gardens outside. They hold various special events, such as all-night camp-ins which enthral children 8–11 (£25 inc science shows, treasure hunts, workshops and breakfast – must bring a snack and a sleeping bag). Meals, snacks, shop, disabled access; cl 24–26 Dec; (020) 7942 4000; free.

Tower of London (Tower Hill) Picturesque classic castle, the most notable building to survive the Great Fire of London. A lot of fun to look at even superficially, it dates back to the late 11th c, though the site had been used as a defensive position by the Romans much earlier. Almost every period of English history has witnessed gruesome goings-on here, with not even the highest or mightiest safe from imprisonment or even execution: Walter Ralegh, Lady Jane Grey and two of Henry VIII's wives spent their last days in the Tower. There's a mass of things to see, inc enough medieval weaponry and armour to glut the appetite of even the most bloodthirsty, and not forgetting the Beefeaters and the ravens – you need a fair bit of time to see everything properly. The Jewel House shows off the Crown Jewels to dazzling effect; on the busiest days those tempted to linger are gently drawn along by moving floorways. Two towers that were part of Edward I's medieval palace are furnished in period style, and peopled with appropriately costumed helpful guides; one room in this part has been left untouched to show what a difficult job the restoration was. A reorganisation of the oldest part, the White Tower, has revealed that the inside of the fortress when built was much less imposing than was suggested by the formidable exterior – they were clearly just trying to intimidate the locals. You can also walk along the elevated battlements. Meals, snacks, shop, some disabled access; cl 24–26 Dec, 1 Jan; (020) 7709 0765; £11.30.

Ragged School Museum (Copperfield Rd, Mile End – a walk from Limehouse station on the Docklands Light Railway, which is the nicest way of getting around this part of London) A neat contrast to the Tower, this canalside warehouse was one of the many 'ragged' (or free) schools set up by Dr Barnardo in Tower Hamlets in the late 19th c. Displays concentrate on the school's history (there's a re-created Victorian classroom), life in the East End in the 1890s, and the work of the great philanthropist himself. An exhibition takes a detailed look at the area's social history over the last 200 years or so, through the eyes of local people inc a former waiter, and an usherette from the People's Palace theatre. Snacks, shop, disabled access to ground floor exhibition only; open Weds, Thurs, and pm first Sun of month (cl Christmas and New Year); (020) 8980 6405; free.

Museum of London (London Wall; Barbican tube station) No other city museum in the world is quite as comprehensive as this; anyone with just a passing interest in history will find it compelling. London's development is told through chronological reconstructions and period clothes, music and various remains, from a medieval hen's egg to an early (and quite different) tube map – ever heard of the station called Post Office? The 18th-, 19th- and 20th-c sections have almost too much to take in. Excellent redeveloped galleries cover Roman London (the building adjoins a stretch of original Roman wall), remarkable research on a 14th-c Black Death cemetery nr the Tower of London, the rich historical clues that have emerged from a Tudor rubbish dump, and, in a new gallery 125 years of history from the French Revolution to World War I. Meals, snacks, shop, disabled access; cl Sun am, 24–26 Dec; (020) 7600 0807; £5 – ticket valid for a year, and it certainly is the sort of place you would want to come back to; children free.

Museum of Childhood (Cambridge Heath Rd, Bethnal Green) This very special little museum houses the V&A's collection of toys, dolls, dolls' houses, games, puppets and children's costumes. Excellent programme of events, theatre shows, and children's activities (most wknds and several school hols) – most completely free. Snacks, shop, disabled access; cl Fri, 24–26 Dec, 1 Jan; (020) 8980 2415; free.

Firepower (Royal Arsenal West, Warren Lane, Woolwich) In the restored former Ministry of Defence research buildings, and part of the overall redevelopment of the Royal Arsenal, this new museum brings to life the history of artillery since Roman times: plenty of big guns and military vehicles, alongside a unique collection of uniforms, photographs, books and manuscripts. Lots to appeal to families, with interactive displays and so forth (the rifle simulator is especially good fun, and an audio-visual show gives an idea what it felt like to be in the middle of a battle), but some of the exhibitions have a more personal side to them, with recorded recollections of former servicemen and women, and a poignant display of medals. Meals, snacks, shop, disabled access; cl 25 Dec; (020) 8855 7755; £6.50.

London Canal Museum (12–13 New Wharf Rd, King's

Cross) The history of London's canal network is told in this former ice warehouse, with newly reworked displays about the people who strove to make a meagre livelihood by living and working on them, the horses which pulled their boats, and the cargoes they carried. You can peer down into a huge ice well, where winter ice was once stored into summer. Temporary exhibitions; book and gift shop; cl Mon exc bank hols, plus 24–26, 31 Dec; (020) 7713 0836; £2.50. A visit here is nicely combined with a trip on the canal. Jason's in Little Venice run enjoyable trips to Camden; (020) 7286 3428; £6.95 return.

Imperial War Museum (Lambeth Rd; Lambeth North tube, or not too far to walk from Westminster) This top-notch museum uses very up-to-date presentation techniques to give a vibrant and sometimes even nerve-wracking exploration of aspects of all wars involving Britain and the Commonwealth since 1914. The Blitz Experience vividly re-creates London's darkest days, and a Trench Experience gives World War I the same treatment. The tone isn't all gung-ho: the interesting archive recordings of people's experiences of war can leave a deep impression, as do some of the harrowing paintings by official war artists. A permanent exhibition on the Holocaust covers much of a six-storey extension. Using original artefacts (many of them lent from former concentration camps) inc a funeral cart from the Warsaw ghetto, letters written by an eight-year-old French Jewish boy before his betrayal and deportation to Auschwitz, and a section of a deportation railcar from Belgium, as well as photographs and the testimony of survivors, it is the largest and most moving memorial to the victims of the Holocaust in the country. Also excellent changing exhibitions; meals, snacks, shop, disabled access; cl 24–26 Dec; (020) 7416 5000; £6.50, free after 4.30pm. It's housed in the former lunatic asylum known as Bedlam, the name a corruption of Bethlehem: the site was originally a hostel set up in the 13th c by the bishop of that town.

There's a clutch of useful tapas bars and the like up past here, around the junction of Kennington Rd and Kennington Lane, and on Waterloo Rd the Fire Station does good food.

Horniman Museum (London Rd, Forest Hill) The new extension to this art nouveau building, to open in Spring 2002, will house their eclectic, mainly ethnographic, collections with artefacts from every continent. Although some galleries will be closed to the public as work continues, the African Worlds gallery (inc a fine group of mummies and Africa's largest mask), the Natural History gallery (lots of stuffed animals), and a recently revamped aquarium will be among those that stay open. In autumn 2002 the remarkable musical instrument collection should have been rehoused – interactive computers will let you hear what some of the extraordinary instruments sound like. Other improvements will include better disabled access, a new café, and a new entrance to the museum from the delightful gardens (with friendly small farm animals). Children love it, despite the old-fashioned feel; good programme of events. Cl Sun am, and 24–26 Dec; (020) 8699 1872; free.

Greenwich

National Maritime Museum (Romney Rd) Enclosed by a spectacular glass canopy roof, this is now one of the country's most impressive museums. The 20 galleries (four new ones added in 2001 inc Prince Frederick's gilded Royal barge among their exhibits) have displays on topics as diverse as passengers, piracy and, of course, sea power; yet another gallery, on oceans and the environment, will open in 2002. Hundreds of exhibits range from contemporary art and great masterpieces of naval battles, to hands-on activities, Nelson's bloodstained coat, and even hardy yachtsman Tony Bullimore's survival suit; you can see some of the thousands of exhibits not on display on computers. Meals, snacks, shop, disabled access; cl 25–26 Dec; (020) 8312 6565; free.

Royal Observatory Greenwich (Greenwich Park) The original home of Greenwich Mean Time – standing as it does on the Prime Meridian of longitude zero. The brass line marking the meridian is still there set in the ground: standing over it with one foot in the western hemisphere and one in the east is irresistible. The Wren-built observatory was founded by Charles II in 1675, and now houses a comprehensive collection of historic instruments for time-keeping, navigation and astronomy. Good views from the top. The Time Ball is rather confusing – it can go down and up so fast you barely notice it. Meals, snacks, shop; cl 24–26 Dec; (020) 8858 4422; free.

Greenwich Park Wonderful views from this carefully landscaped park sloping down towards the river; it's a great place for a picnic. A herd of deer grazes in a smallish area of woodland and wild flowers known as the Wilderness, and there's the largest children's playground in any Royal Park (as well as the preserved trunk of a tree in which the young Elizabeth I is said to have played).

You should be able to get boat trips from the pier up to Westminster (around £7.50), and a route booklet from the Tourist Information Centre (£2) lets you follow one of five Millennium Heritage Trails – a pleasant way to spend a sunny afternoon.

The Cutty Sark (Lassell St) and Trafalgar (Park Row) are good river-view dining pubs.

South-West England & Southern Wales

Including Cornwall, Devon, Dorset, Gloucestershire, Somerset, and also Herefordshire, the southern part of Shropshire, and Worcestershire

SEE MAP 2

◆ ◆ ◆

1. Pan for silver and explore the forest

Llywernog Silver Lead Mine (A434 just W of Ponterwyd) A lively place, set against a beautiful sweeping mountainside backdrop. Regular displays of silver panning, sound and light tableaux in the caves and tunnels along the expanded underground tour, and working water-wheels; you can try panning for fool's gold or dowsing for mineral veins. Wear sensible shoes in wet weather. Snacks, shop, some disabled access; open mid-Mar to Oct (cl Mon exc July–Aug); (01970) 890620; £4.95.

Bwlch Nant-yr-Arian Forest Centre (A44 just W) Designated Kite Country centre, with feeding daily all year (3pm summer, 2pm winter). Explore the forest on the scenic way-marked walks and enjoy breathtaking valley views. There's a new mountain bike trail and a lakeside walk even wheelchairs can manage. Visitor centre (01970) 890694, with snacks, shop, disabled access; picnic areas and children's play area; cl 25 Dec. Free (parking £1).

2. St David's – plenty of family fun

Although grown-ups will want to see the cathedral, children will have much more fun exploring the impressive ruins of the **Bishop's Palace**, clearly once very grand: plenty of quadrangles, stairways and splendid arcaded walls, with all sorts of intricate and often entertaining details (like the carvings below the arcaded parapets). Atmospheric and tranquil, particularly out of season when you may have it largely to yourself. Shop, limited disabled access; cl am winter Suns, 24-26 Dec, 1 Jan; (01437) 720517; £2; Cadw.

Oceanarium (New St) Excellent insight into sea and shore life; highlights include the shark tank and rock pool. Talks and demonstrations for children during school hols. Snacks, shop, limited disabled access; cl 24–26 Dec; (01437) 720453; £3.

St David's Farm Park (NE edge, off A487) Commercial farm with rare breed animals as well, and a network of grassy paths giving a view into most fields; playgrounds and picnic areas. Normally cl only Nov–Mar; (01437) 721601; £2 suggested donation.

St David's is a good area for coastal walks, perhaps to ancient sites such as the neolithic burial chambers up by St David's Head to the S or over towards Solva, to St Non's Chapel, or W to St Justinian (another chapel here, looking over Ramsey Island). The Old Cross Hotel nr the cathedral is a civilised place for lunch, and the cheerful Farmers Arms is good value. The beach at Whitesands Bay is good. In summer there are boat trips from the lifeboat station to rocky Ramsey Island, where seabirds nest in great numbers.

Adventure Days organise well supervised abseiling, canoeing, rock-climbing and other activities – ideal for off-loading active children for the day (over-8s only); (01437) 721611.

3. A bouncy theme park

Oakwood (A4075 W of Narberth) The only real theme park in Wales, and a good one too, especially in the summer hols when they stay open till 10pm, rounding off every night with a firework display and lightshow. There's a real mix of things to do, from Europe's biggest wooden roller-coaster to live Mississippi showboat shows. Younger children have their own little roller-coaster (there's another medium-sized one aimed at families), and carousels and the like. The real talking point is the sky-coaster, Vertigo: you're strapped in a harness and winched to a height of up to 50 metres (165 ft), then free-fall at 70mph back towards the ground – just in time you'll start swinging like a frantic pendulum. A nightmare cross between bungee-jumping and a parachute drop, this obviously wouldn't suit everyone, so rather than bump up the entry price, there's an extra charge (£30 for up to three people, the maximum number that can go on it at once). This has proved enormously popular, so if you want to try it in peak periods you'll need to get there fairly early to book in. Meals, snacks, shop, disabled access; cl Oct–Easter (exc school hols); (0845) 3455667; £11.75.

The Angel in Narberth has good food.

4. A wonderful place to wander through

Stackpole Estate & Bosherston Lakes E of Bosherston, this spectacular 2,000-acre estate is a real delight to wander through, with lily ponds, woodlands, cliffs, dunes and beaches offering a range of landscapes to suit every taste and mood. Bosherston Lakes make a particularly easy strolling-ground, with level paths around them; a fine sight when the lilies are in bloom in summer; several car parks; free. At the S end you can cross dunes to emerge on to a large sandy beach, Broad Haven. Barafundle Bay is a lovely relatively undiscovered beach. Snacks (at Stackpole Quay); (01646) 661359; car park open Easter–Sept, £1.80 (free to NT members); NT.

The Armstrong Arms does good food, and the St Govan's pub is useful too.

5. Tenby – boat trips, dinosaurs and a spooky cave

Caldey Island boat trips Reached by summer boat trips from Tenby harbour (Apr–Sept, weather permitting, £7), still a monastic island, where the Cistercian monks have good creamy chocolate for sale, as well as more durable crafts and old-fashioned perfume. Besides the modern abbey, there's a 13th-c church with a simple cobbled floor, still in use, on one side of the small cloister of the original priory; these ancient priory buildings (which you can see from outside but not enter) give a better sense of the past than almost anywhere else in West Wales. Sailing times from the Tourist Information Centre, (01834) 842404.

Dinosaur Park (Great Wedlock Farm, Gumfreston – B4318 W) Family-run, in a rural setting: over 20 life-size dinosaurs in glades and swamps along a woodland trail; outdoor and indoor adventure playgrounds, an organised daily activity programme, pets, rides, and computer games. Restaurant, indoor and outdoor snack kiosks, and picnic facilities, shop, disabled access; open daily Easter–Sept, and wkdys Oct; (01834) 845272; £3.95.

Hoyle's Mouth Cave (off A4139 just SW, Trefloyne Lane towards St Florence; short path through wood on left after 500 yds) Running more than 30 metres (100 ft) back into the hillside, this spooky place has yielded Ice Age mammoth bones, as well as human tools dating back over 10,000 years. Take a torch, but don't go in winter – you'd disturb the hibernating bats.

Tenby is a pleasantly restrained family seaside resort, with sheltered beaches and rock coves. It's a walled town, the splendidly preserved 13th-c wall still with many of its towers left, as well as a magnificent 14th-c arched barbican gateway; a moat used to run the whole length of what is now a tree-lined street.

The medieval Plantagenet House has good interesting food.

6. Margam Park

(A48, SE of Port Talbot) Pretty country park based around a splendid gothick mansion, its 850 acres full of natural and historic features and various themed areas, inc a scaled-down nursery-rhyme village for young children. Also a ruined abbey and Iron Age hill fort, marked walks among the parkland and forests, giant maze, deer and cattle, and an adventure playground. Meals, snacks, shop, disabled access; usually cl winter Mon and Tues, 25 Dec; (01639) 881635; £3.85, £1 in winter when none of the attractions is open (though they have various special events).

7. Big Pit Mining Museum

(B4248, Blaenavon) Whoever said you can't get something for nothing had obviously never been on one of these unforgettable colliery tours; they've been outstanding for years, but since the site became part of the National Museum of Wales they've been completely free, for adults and children. This was a working pit for 200 years, until 1980, and the tour guides are all former miners; it's partly their anecdotes and expertise that make it so evocative, but of course there's also something unique about the atmosphere underground. There are plenty of colliery workings to explore on the surface, but it's the hour-long pit tours that stand out; armed with a hard hat and lamp, you get into the pit cage and descend 90 metres (300 ft) into the inky blackness that was daily life for generations of local men. It's quite a shock trying to adjust to the light from your helmet; the guides work hard to make everyone feel comfortable, but if you're particularly averse to confined spaces then this isn't for you. Lots of information about the industry is packed in, and you'll get far more of a feel for the realities of the industry than you ever could above ground. Wrap up warm (even in summer) and wear sensible footwear. They don't allow children under 5, or anyone under a metre tall. Back on the surface there's a reconstructed miner's cottage, and an exhibition in the old pithead baths. The whole site takes around two and a half hours to see properly. Meals, snacks, shop, disabled access (even underground, though you must book); usually cl Nov–Feb, though it is worth checking then; (01495) 790311; free.

8. Welsh life through the ages

Museum of Welsh Life (St Fagans, A4232 4m W of Cardiff) Excellent 100-acre open-air museum, with a variety of reconstructed buildings illustrating styles and living conditions throughout the ages. Buildings have come from all over Wales, and there are some remarkable exhibits, inc a homely gas-lit Edwardian farmhouse and an entire Celtic village. You can buy things from a period grocery store. Also crafts and lots of seasonal events – there's plenty to fascinate here. Meals and snacks (in 1920s tearoom), shop, limited disabled access; cl 24–25 Dec; (029) 2057 3500; free.

The Plymouth Arms is very handy for good value food.

9. Cardiff's reborn waterfront

Cardiff Bay Visitor Centre (Bute St) This space-age-style centre explains the ambitious continuing rejuvenation of Cardiff's waterfront and docklands; cl 24-26 Dec; (029) 2046 3833; free. The heart of the development is an ornamental lagoon, created by flooding a vast tract of mudflats, involving a 1,000-metre barrage (and a cost of £191 million). Mermais Quay, the focal point of the Bay, with its cafés, restaurants and shops leading down to the waterfront, Techniquest, and a re-created Norwegian seaman's timbered church, are just some of the rather miscellaneous group of buildings and attractions clustered around the magnificent old Pierhead building. The docklands New Sea Lock (Harrowby St) may be Cardiff's most unspoilt pub, the smarter Wharf (Atlantic Wharf) is right on the water's edge. In theory, two key tracts of wasteland are earmarked for showpiece new buildings here, one the Wales Millennium Centre arts complex to house the Welsh National Opera, and the other an ostentatiously futuristic glass-covered debating chamber for the Welsh Assembly. In practice both projects have been dogged by serious difficulties (in summer 2001 the debating chamber architect and the assembly fell out amidst mutual accusations of mismanagement, after projected costs soared from £27 to £47 million). So we no longer believe projected completion dates late in 2002.

Techniquest (Stuart St) An excellent family excursion, with fun as well as interest at this hi-tech science centre; around 160 hands-on exhibits and activities, and a planetarium – all exceptionally well done. Meals, snacks, shop, very good disabled access; cl 24–26 Dec; (029) 2047 5475; *£6.30.

Craft in the Bay (Bute St) Demonstrations by potters, jewellers and glass workers, and a large gallery and shop; cl 25-26 Dec, 1 Jan; free.

Away from the waterfront, Cardiff's bustling centre has a good friendly feel, with pedestrianised parts (for example around the fine church of St John the Baptist), and several interesting Victorian covered shopping arcades, as well as modern ones. Multi-ride bus tickets are good value for getting around. The Cottage, Prince of Wales (both St Mary St) and Golden Cross (Custom House St) are useful for lunch, and in summer most of the cafés and bars in Mill Lane have outside tables and chairs. Cardiff Castle is nearby, with Capability Brown's 18th-c landscaped park between it and the river. The magnificent riverside Millennium Stadium is also surprisingly central, and on match days the roar of the crowds can be heard right across the city; there are hourly tours every day, (029) 2082 2228; £5. The white neo-classical City Hall, flanked by the National Museum of Wales and the Law Courts, holds itself slightly aloof, and leads to formal Cathays Park, now dominated by the grand buildings of the city's university. The one must-see in here is the **National Museum of Wales** (Cathays Park) Lively, with interactive displays and exhibitions on subjects as diverse as ceramics, coins and prehistoric sea monsters. The East Wing has an impressive collection of paintings, with notable French Impressionists, and there's an excellent section on the evolution of the Welsh landscape. Meals, snacks, shop, disabled access; cl Mon (exc bank hols), 25 Dec; (029) 2039 7951; free.

10. An exciting day in Ironbridge

Ironbridge Gorge Museum Many former industrial sites now make up this outstanding network, one of the most satisfying places to visit in the whole country, scattered over six miles along the gorge. Fifty-acre **Blists Hill** is the highlight, and the part children like best – a complete reconstructed Victorian village, showing everything from the offices, houses and machinery to the school, pubs, pigsties and swingboats; it's the biggest open-air museum of its kind. Costumed staff add authenticity, and there are extra activities in the school hols. The other main sections include museums devoted to the river, and the iron, china and tile-making industries, with some beautifully restored houses (and wonderful echoes in the brick kilns at Coalport) and a former clay tobacco pipe factory in Broseley. You need buy tickets only for the parts you're interested in (useful leaflets suggest a variety of itineraries, from three hours to a whole day), but a special offer Passport Ticket covering everything is good value – and remains valid indefinitely until you've seen all the bits you want. On bank hol Sun and Mon the sites are linked by a bus, otherwise it's best to drive (or walk). Meals, snacks, shops, disabled access; cl 24–25 Dec, 1 Jan and some parts cl Nov–Mar – best to ring first then; (01952) 432166; £10 Passport ticket, or individual tickets to each museum available – Blists Hill is £7.50.

Attractively placed by the riverside in Ironbridge, the Meadow, Olde Robin Hood and particularly the Malthouse are all good lunch stops. The Boat at Jackfield and Shakespeare at Coalport are handy for Maws craft centre and the Coalport Museum. There's a pleasant terraced walk between the river and the Golden Ball (Wesley Rd, off Madeley Hill). For a fuller restaurant meal, the Coracle in the square is nice. The River Severn passes through a partly wooded gorge along here, and there are plenty of good places for strolling.

11. Shropshire country life

Secret Hills Discovery Centre (A49 just S of Craven Arms) Another of the Millennium Commission's projects, this grass-roofed structure in 25 acres of meadows takes a fresh look at the natural and cultural history of the surrounding countryside. Various galleries house interactive exhibitions on topics as diverse as the geology of landscape, and the art and music it's inspired. A simulated balloon ride over the hills should amuse children, and other attractions include a full-size model of a mammoth skeleton, and craft workshops. Restaurant, shop, good disabled access; probably cl mid-Dec–mid-Jan but phone to check; (01588) 676000; £4.25.

Acton Scott Historic Working Farm (Acton Scott, off A49) Vivid introduction to traditional rural life, with plenty of rare breeds, and crops cultivated using old rotation methods; all the work is done by hand or horse power, with period farm machinery. Lots of craft demonstrations, and daily butter-making. Unusually, this is a farm aimed just as much at adults (maybe more) as at children. Meals, snacks, shop, disabled access; cl Mon (exc bank hols), and Nov–Mar; (01694) 781306; £3.95. The handiest place for lunch is the Ragleth in Little Stretton.

12. Wildlife and woodland walks around a traditional farm

Rays Farm Country Matters (Billingsley) Traditional farm in pleasant countryside, with sheep, horses and cattle and llamas, a good collection of owls and plenty of red and fallow deer; they also have otters. Pleasant woodland walks, sculpture trail and indoor and outdoor picnic areas. They have atmospheric activities in the run-up to Christmas. Snacks, shop, disabled access; cl Jan, and wkdys in Feb till half-term; (01299) 841255; £4. For longer walks, you can try a section of bridleway starting at the farm, meandering eventually into Wales.

Stations for the Severn Valley Railway are quite close, at Hampton and at Highley (where the Ship Inn gives access to Severnside walks).

13. Owls and miniature animals

Small Breeds Farm Park and Owl Centre (off A4111 S of Kington) Friendly little farm with rare and unusual miniature horses, donkeys, goats, poultry, pheasants and waterfowl, as well as a family of playful chipmunks and a pair of kune kune pigs. They like children to get their hands on things here, all the animals can be shown under cover if it's raining, and there's a heated barn for picnics. The views and setting are a bonus, and the fantastic collections of owls and waterfowl are set in an attractively landscaped garden. Snacks, shop, disabled access; open daily Easter–end Oct, plus most winter wknds but ring to check; (01544) 231109; *£3.50.

Nearby Kington is an attractive border town by the River Arrow, well placed for walks, with some intriguing bric-a-brac and craft shops. The Queens Head has good value food. The long-distance Offa's Dyke Path passes through town, descending into it from Hergest Ridge, NW Herefordshire's answer to the Malverns; at the far end across the Welsh border the ridge tapers into horseback width above Gladestry, while N of Kington the path goes along one of the best-preserved stretches of Offa's Dyke.

14. A friendly stately home

Berrington Hall (A49, Ashton) This elegant 18th-c house has some activities that make it a reliable bet for families. There are a good few quiz sheets and trails to follow going round the house (50p extra), some designed for under-7s, others for older children, as well as an I Spy sheet (10p) for the beautifully laid out grounds. The house itself has lots of interest; the finely painted ceilings and Regency furnishings are memorably elegant, and the main stairway is splendid. Many rooms are furnished in a way that lets you think they are still in use: there's a fully equipped Victorian nursery and a tiled dairy. Also a good adventure playground and a children's orienteering course, and plenty of walks and pathways. Capability Brown laid out the grounds (the house was built by his son-in-law); the most famous feature is the 14-acre lake with picturesque views, but there's also an attractive woodland garden, and rows of yew trees. The walled garden has some venerable apple trees.

Meals, snacks, shop, some disabled access; open pm Sat–Weds from Apr to Oct, though the shop and restaurant are also open wknds up to Christmas; (01568) 615721; £4.30 (£2.10 children).

The Stockton Cross Inn (A4112) is a nice old place for lunch, but doesn't take under-6s. Other nearby places we can recommend are the Boot at Orleton and (more up-market) the Roebuck at Brimfield.

15. Eastnor Castle

(A438 just E of Ledbury) This splendid neo-Gothic structure is just what you want a castle to look like, with stirring battlements and exaggerated towers, and some breathtakingly extravagant rooms. It was begun in 1812, its grand scale soon brought visitors bringing to look; it's still very much a family home. The attractions specifically designed for children are in the grounds, but they can get a lot of pleasure from the house itself; designed by Pugin, the richly furnished and decorated rooms are quite atmospheric – particularly the red hall. The wonderfully over the top drawing room is another highlight, as is the great hall. You can get children's worksheets to keep up interest. The attractive grounds have an arboretum, 300-acre deer park, plenty of space for a picnic or exploring, and a garden centre, but what younger visitors enjoy most is the growing yew hedge maze, reached through a door next to the till in the garden shop. There are three trails to make it more fun as you go round (one based around Harry Potter); if you solve the clues you get a lolly at the end. They also have a rope maze, and Nine Man's Morris. In mid-Aug they usually have a week with extra children's activities. You can stay in the house for the full castle experience (they have 11 unique bedrooms). The outside looks especially dramatic in autumn, when the Virginia creeper that all but envelops the walls turns a fierce red. Dogs on a lead are welcome in the grounds. Meals, snacks, shop; open Sun and bank hols mid-Apr–early Oct, daily (exc Sat) July and Aug; (01531) 633160; £5 adults (£3 garden only), £3 children (£2 garden only) – the maze (run separately by the garden centre) is an extra 95p, or £3 for families.

In Ledbury, which has a remarkably well stocked Playmobile specialist just off the main st, the Market Place Restaurant (Homend) is good value, as are bar lunches in the smart old Feathers Hotel.

16. Severn Valley Railway

(Bewdley) Run with real verve, this is probably Britain's leading standard-gauge steam railway, and the showpiece station here has been splendidly restored. Its 16 miles pass through more than one county, between Kidderminster at this end and Bridgnorth at the other. If you simply wanted to go straight there and straight back, the full return journey takes around 2½ hours, but it's much more fun to base a day around it, getting off at the various little stations on the way, and having a leisurely stroll around the villages and surrounding countryside (there are plenty of well marked footpaths and riverside walks). The line was built between 1858 and 1862, and was never financially successful; it's been preserved thanks to the dedication of hundreds of unpaid volunteers, who you'll see working each wknd on the stock or stations. You can usually watch work on some of the fine old carriages in the yard at Bewdley, which also has a good model railway. You don't have to be a steam buff to enjoy the journey; the route largely follows the Severn, and the views are delightful. As there aren't too many roads in the valley, the train is the only way of seeing some parts of the unspoilt countryside. You'll cross a particularly dramatic single-span 60-metre (200-ft) bridge. Most of the trains have refreshment cars, and there are cafés in the stations at Bewdley, Kidderminster and Bridgnorth (which also has a notable collection of locomotives). They have various special events, inc Santa Specials in the run-up to Christmas; you may find different fares and trains then. Trains run wknds all year, and usually daily May–Sept and in school hols; (01299) 403816 for timetable. A full return fare allows unlimited travel that day, getting on or off as you please; £9.60 adults, £4.80 children 5–15. A family ticket, covering two adults and four children, is £25.

17. West Midlands Safari Park

(A456 just E of Bewdley) Very much a full day out, with the main attraction the drive-round animal reserves, home to over 40 species of rare and exotic animals; you can go round as often as you like. Admission covers the entertaining sea lion show, a seal aquarium, reptile house and pets corner, but you'll have to pay extra for the leisure park, which has around 30 rides from gentle carousels to a roller-coaster and popular log flume. Lots of differently themed shops and places to eat. Meals, snacks, shop, mostly disabled access; open daily Apr–end Oct; (01299) 402114; the safari park is £5.95 for adults and children over 4; this entitles you to a return visit during the rest of the season. At the leisure park, rides are priced individually, or an all-day wristband is £7.

Bewdley is an attractive small town, with riverside walks and interesting side streets. The Little Pack Horse (old High St) has good value food and is full of character.

18. Refuge for endangered buildings

Avoncroft Museum of Historic Buildings (2m S of Bromsgrove at Stoke Prior, by A38 bypass and B4091) An enjoyable place to spend a relaxing afternoon. Around 25 buildings from the last seven centuries have been saved from demolition and rebuilt here: there's a timber-framed merchant's house, a Victorian church and gaol, even a 1946 prefab. A lovely working windmill is particularly popular with children, and, more incongruously, there's a unique collection of telephone kiosks, from Tardis-style police boxes to today's horrible glass ones, with everything in between. Also a play area, and there are donkeys, a goat and chickens wandering about. Several of the buildings are furnished inside, but it's very much a place to visit on a dry day, when children can make the most of the open space the museum stands on. Meals, snacks, picnic area, shop, disabled access; cl Mon (exc July and Aug), Fri in Nov and Mar, and all Dec–Feb; (01527) 831363; £5.

The nearby Country Girl has enjoyable food, and is handy for walks on Dodderhill Common.

19. A Worcester day out

Commandery (Sidbury) Lively museum wholly devoted to the English Civil War, in striking timber-framed 15th-c building. Lots of weaponry, spectacular audio-visual shows and life-size talking figures re-creating events from the war. Unusual special events and historic military displays. Meals, snacks, shop; cl am Sun, 25–26 Dec, 1 Jan; (01905) 361821; £3.60.

While you're in the town, it's worth popping into the **Museum of Local Life** (Friar St) This 15th-c building houses an interesting museum of local life, with events such as children's workshops. Shop with reproduction nostalgiamenta, disabled access to ground floor only; cl Thurs, Sun, 25–26 Dec, 1 Jan, Good Fri; (01905) 722349; free.

In the same street the Lemon Tree (Friar St) has good food, and in New St the King Charles does good meals.

Bennetts Farm Park (Lower Wick, SW of city) Working dairy farm with animals, wknd milking parlour and vintage machinery museum in pretty 16th-c farm buildings. Walks and fishing in season. Cl Sept–Easter, snacks (inc their own ice cream), shop; (01905) 748102; £2.

Worcester Woods Country Park (just E off A442) Ancient woodland and wildflower meadows with circular walks, trails and map-reading games – a real taste of the country for Worcester folk; also play and picnic areas and a visitor centre (cl 25–26 Dec, 1 Jan; free). Meals, snacks, shop, disabled access.

The Swan at nearby Whittington has good value food.

20. The Forest of Dean

The Forest of Dean is a unique landscape: hilly woodland that shows many traces of the way it has provided a livelihood for the people living around it. Its woodland colours are at their best in late May and autumn. Still largely ancient oak woodland despite encroaching pine plantations, the forest rolls over many miles of hilly countryside, giving plenty of space – even in summer you can often have much of the woods to yourself. There are ponds, streams with stepping stones, cattle and maybe fallow deer. There are also ancient iron workings, the tracks of abandoned railways and tramways, and still one or two of the freeminers, who've been digging coal by hand from surface seams for hundreds of years. The forest scenery has most impact on those prepared to delve into its past a bit. A good start is the **Dean Heritage Centre** (Camp Mill, Upper Soudley), set around an old watermill in a pretty wooded valley. Plenty going on, inc a beam engine, a collection of clocks all made by a local family, craft displays, adventure playground, and occasional traditional charcoal burning. Meals, snacks, shop, disabled access; cl 24–26 Dec and 1 Jan; (01594) 822170; *£4.

The forest is well equipped with car parks, picnic sites and forest trails. The **Sculpture Trail** takes a four-mile route passing nearly 20 specially commissioned sculptures hidden deep in the forest (starting from picnic site nr the comfortable Speech House Hotel). The **Kidnalls Forest Trail** is a good way of tracking down some early industrial sites. The **Foundry Wood Trail** passes Soudley fish ponds and gains some fine views. The **Wench Ford Forest Walk** leads past a series of quite interesting rock outcrops. Signed paths ensure easy route-finding up to the open summit of May Hill, where on a clear day you can see the Cotswolds, Malverns, Welsh Marches and Severn estuary. Around the edges of the forest the scenery changes to a patchwork of steep pastures – also very attractive. It's well worth getting a forest map, either from the Dean Heritage Centre or direct from the Forestry Commission in Coleford (01594) 833057; these outline walks (inc the sculpture trail), and mark the best spots for views or picnics. The information centres can also provide details of canoeing, caving, cycling or fishing in the forest.

Symonds Yat Rock Perhaps the Forest of Dean's most spectacular feature, where the River Wye rolls around a monumental wooded cliff barrier, a favourite spot with peregrine falcons; tremendous views in all directions from the top, and at the bottom a 60p ferry crosses the river from the popular Saracens Head Inn, which has plenty of tables out on waterside terraces (and summer boat trips).

21. Hawking and Victorian life

National Birds of Prey Centre (Great Boulsdon, just S of Newent) Exceptional collection of 81 species of birds of prey, with flying displays and breeding aviaries, also picnic and play areas. Meals, snacks, shop, some disabled access; cl Dec, Jan (exc for special events); (01531) 821581; £5.75.

The Yew Tree at Cliffords Mesne a bit further on this road has decent food; it is on the slopes of May Hill, which is owned by the National Trust and has some scope for walking.

Shambles Museum of Victorian Life (Church St, Newent) Enthusiastic re-creation of Victorian cobbled square, with shops and furnished tradesman's house. Summer snacks, shop, limited disabled access; cl Mon (exc bank hols), Jan–mid-Mar; (01531) 822144; £3.50.

The George opposite is a nice old coaching inn with good value lunchtime food, and the little town has some attractive timbered buildings.

22. Waterfront action, countryside peace

National Waterways Museum (Llanthony Warehouse, Gloucester Docks) Focusing on the history of Britain's network of inland waterways, this has quite an emphasis on hands-on exhibits, with lots of touch-screen activities ranging from building your own canal, to an infuriating share certificate game where you're allocated a company and then follow its fortunes. Elsewhere, a highlight is the miniature lock chamber, where you can try steering a narrow boat through the locks. One gallery looks at the way boats have been decorated from ancient times. Most displays are under cover, though there are some historic boats outside, and in summer (for an extra charge), you can take 45-min boat trips along the canal or river trips as far as Tewkesbury. There are special events during the school holidays, and usually a fully working traditional forge. Snacks, shop, disabled access (not to floating exhibits); cl 25 Dec; (01452) 318054; £4.95 (£3.95 children over 5). They do family tickets that include a boat trip as well: £22 for two adults and three children.

Gloucester's revitalised waterfront deserves much of the credit for the city's tourism renaissance, and the guided walks are interesting. Other attractions here include the unusually interesting **Soldiers of Gloucester Museum** which has life-size reconstructions inc a World War I trench; (cl winter Mon); (01452) 522682; £4), and a big antiques centre, with 110 varied antique shops in Dickensian arcades (limited disabled access; cl am Sun; free wkdys, 50p wknds and bank hols).

The Waterfront (Llanthony Rd, S end of docks) and Tall Ship (docks entrance) are useful for a quick lunch.

Robinswood Hill Country Park (2m S of Gloucester) A little outcrop of the Cotswolds, with 250 acres of walks and trails, a wildlife information centre (fun talks and events), and wonderful views of the city from the summit, with plenty of places for picnics. Snacks, shop, disabled access; (01452) 303206; free.

23. One of Britain's best farm parks

Cotswold Farm Park (off B4077, Kineton) Popular with readers, this friendly place is full of delightfully odd-looking species of sheep, cattle, pigs, goats, horses and poultry. It's very much a working farm rather than a more developed leisure attraction, but is particularly well organised as far as children are concerned, and excellent value too. Rabbits and guinea pigs to cuddle or feed, tractor and trailer rides, battery powered tractors for 3–12-yr-olds, good safe rustic-themed play areas and even a designated children's shop. Try to visit close to the start of the season (up to end Apr), when the lambs are being born. Audio tours are available for adults; nature trails and woodland walks are ideal for a break from the animals, and there are 19 acres where you can have a picnic or relax on the grass. Lots under cover, so still good when the weather isn't perfect (best to wear wellies then). Meals, snacks, shop, disabled access; open mid-Mar–Sept (ring for opening times in Oct); (01451) 850307; £4.50 (children £2.50). A family ticket is £13.

25. Wildfowl & Wetlands Trust

(Slimbridge, off A38) The original and best of the Trust's nine centres, this enormous place is one of the most visitor-friendly bird reserves in the country, with plenty of activities aimed specifically at primary school children. It's been considerably upgraded in recent years (thanks in part to a hefty grant from the Millennium Commission); there's a very impressive new visitor centre, and much improved restaurant and shop. Showing off probably the world's most comprehensive collection of geese, swans and ducks, this is the only place in Europe where you can see six species of flamingo, as well as plenty of other rare and wild birds, and a tropical house that re-creates the sights, sounds and smells of a rain forest. In the Pond Zone children can learn about wetland environments by taking part in pond-dipping and seeing the things they fish out of the water magnified on TV screens. Lots of touch screen computers, video displays and games, and extra events and activities in the school holidays, inc special trails and face-painting; on summer wknds they may have Land Rover safaris. Other highlights include an impressive discovery centre, a tower with a telescope (great views of the River Severn), sculpture trail, and a wildlife art gallery; there's also a small play area. It's unusual in being somewhere that you might get more out of visiting in winter, when up to 8,000 wild birds fly in; several of the excellent hides and viewing facilities are heated then. Some birds can be fed by hand, and you may be lucky enough to hear the amazing belch of the macoa duck. They'll hire out binoculars if you've left your own at home. Meals, snacks, shop, disabled access; cl 25 Dec; (01453) 890333; £6 adults, £3.60 children over 4, free to WWT members; a family ticket is £15.60.

The Tudor Arms by the swing bridge across the canal is useful for food, and the village Post Office has details of pleasant little walks.

26. Bristol's exciting harbourside

The docks are now largely restored, with distinctive blue and yellow ferries (Apr-Sept) linking several points. The old part around King St, between the waterfront and the Bristol Old Vic, has quiet cobbled streets of Georgian buildings, pleasant to wander through, and elsewhere some of the bigger warehouses (and even the boats) have been pressed into service as museums, café-bars and the like. The Arnolfini, a big former tea warehouse, is now a contemporary arts complex with bar, restaurant, exhibitions, cinema, theatre and so forth.

@Bristol (Harbourside) Explore is the part to head for if your time is limited: full of interactive and hands-on features, it lets you star in your own TV show, play virtual volleyball, or get an idea of how it feels to be in the eye of a tornado. The latest technology gives a new spin to time-honoured activities like generating electricity or making things fly, and there are novelties like the virtual sperm journey and the walk-in womb. Especially good is the Imaginarium, a next-generation planetarium that looks like a metal sphere and takes you into a 3-D virtual universe. There are also workshops, such as on how chocolate is made. Wildwalk is a well put together walk-through journey around evolution, particularly strong on insects, with lots of videos and multi-media bits; its best part is the re-created tropical rain forest, with free-flying birds and butterflies. These sections, and a huge IMAX cinema with a screen four storeys high, are linked by appealingly landscaped squares and avenues, dotted with trees, sculptures, shops and restaurants. Disabled access; cl 25 Dec; (0117) 915 1000; admission for one attraction is £6.50, the All-Star ticket (everything exc Imaginarium) is £15.50.

SS *Great Britain* On the dockside, on some summer wknds a small steam railway will whisk you along the old cargo route to and from this ship, designed by Brunel as the first iron, screw-propelled, ocean-going vessel, and a real departure from what had gone before. Meals, snacks, shop; cl 24-25 Dec; (0117) 926 0680; £6.25. This includes entry to the Maritime Heritage Centre, with reconstructions and original machinery illustrating the city's long history of ship-building. The nearby 1930s diesel-powered firefloat *Pyronaut* and Fairbairn steam-crane (1876) operate on occasional summer wknds.

Historic boat trips (from Princes Wharf) The 1860s steam-tug *Mayflower*, the *Pyronaut* and the tug *John King* give interesting trips round the dock in the summer – best to check times with the Industrial Museum; (0117) 925 1470; *£3. From Apr to Oct the pleasure steamers *Waverley* and *Balmoral* run fairly frequent day cruises from here, along the Avon and Severn or to Devon, Wales or Lundy; (0141) 221 8152 for timetable.

27. Bristol Zoo Gardens

(Clifton Downs; easily reached by buses 8, 9, 508 and 509 from the centre) One of the most enjoyable zoos in the country, excellent value, lots to see, and plenty of well thought out children's activities. Highlights include the Seal and Penguin Coasts, a transparent underwater walkway that offers an unrivalled view of penguins and seals in their natural environment, Bug World, showing creatures like flat-tailed scorpions and moon jellyfish, and Twilight World, with wide-awake nocturnal creatures inc a walk-through bat enclosure. Good adventure playground, activity centre with brass rubbing and face painting, and Zoolympics, a trail around the enclosures that lets children measure their skills and strength against some of the animals. Lots of themed weeks and events. Everything is spread over beautifully laid out gardens, with spacious lawns and colourful borders. Meals, snacks, shop, good disabled access; cl 25 Dec; (0117) 973 8951; £8.40.

28. Bargain Bristol

Create Centre (Smeaton Rd, Spike Island) Lively environmental centre with hands-on displays about recycling, some intriguing exhibits inc a column made from 6½ million cans, and an ecohome (pms only) showcasing methods for greener everyday living. Also changing exhibitions of local art. Shop, café, disabled access; cl most wknds, though best to check; (0117) 925 0505; free.

Bristol Industrial Museum (Princes Wharf) In a converted dockside transit shed, and especially good on transport, with locally built steam locomotives and aircraft (inc a mock-up of Concorde's flight deck), and a good look at the development of the port. Shop, disabled access; open Sat–Weds Apr–Oct, wknds only Nov–Mar; (0117) 925 1470; free. Steam trains run along the docks between here and the SS *Great Britain* every ¼hr 12–5pm on selected days Mar–Oct; £1.

Blaise Castle House Museum (Henbury, 4m NW, off B4047) A spacious and locally popular undulating park with some woodland and refreshments. The late 18th-c house is now a branch of the City Museum, with lots of carefully explained farming equipment, and collections of costume and dolls. The castle itself is a Gothic folly built in 1766 within the now scarcely discernible ramparts of an Iron Age hill fort. Shop, disabled access; museum cl Thurs and Fri, and all Nov–Mar, park open daily; (0117) 950 6789; free. Nearby Blaise Hamlet is a NT-owned estate village designed by John Nash.

29. Horses and hills

Horse World (Staunton Lane, Whitchurch, off A37 S edge of Bristol) A must for horse lovers, this recent development is home to over 200 rescued and retired horses, ponies and donkeys, but what makes it special is the range of other attractions on offer, with plenty to fill a busy half-day. Pleasantly restored farm buildings house an interactive museum examining the origins of the horse and its influence on the human world, a video theatre, friendly and docile donkeys, and an extensive collection of tack and harnesses. There's a twice-daily horse parade (11.30 and 2.30), a nature trail around the paddocks, a horse-themed play area, plenty of space for picnics, and other animals to meet such as goats, lambs, chickens and rabbits. Meals, snacks, shop, disabled access; (01275) 540173. Entry to the site is free, but a self-guided tour (taking in all the areas mentioned above) costs £3.50.

Burrington Combe An easy walk by the B3134 (the best drive through the Mendips), this great steeply wooded limestone gorge on the N flank of the Mendips can be combined with walks up on to Black Down for memorable views in all directions, and over the heather and cranberry tops to Dolebury Warren, where the site of an Iron Age hill fort marks a splendid Mendip viewpoint. Other good starting points for Mendips walks include the Crown at Churchill, Swan at Rowberrow, and Ring o' Bells at Compton Martin.

30. Cheddar Caves and Gorge

(Cheddar) Perhaps a little bustling in summer for some tastes, this busy spot nevertheless boasts two quite remarkable show caves, well worth a look, and it's efficiently organised for families. Even if you balk at the crowds it's a useful way of seeing some of Britain's most extraordinary scenery. The family ticket is good value, and seeing everything included can easily fill half a day, though you'd have to be reasonably fit. The highlight for adults is probably Gough's Cave, named after the retired sea captain who stumbled across it in 1890; this series of stunning underground caverns goes on for around a quarter of a mile, each area seeming more dramatic than the last, with spectacular stalactites and stalagmites joining to form columns. Nearby Cox's Cave is smaller, and more beautifully coloured; no less thrilling, it hasn't got the same spacious grandeur (and has several very narrow passageways). Children should be suitably impressed too, but may prefer the Crystal Quest, another cave entertainingly fitted out with goblins, wizards, and a smoke-filled dragon; a story and challenge lead you through. There's also an exhibition devoted to Cheddar Man, Britain's oldest complete skeleton, with a re-creation of what his world was like, 9,000 years ago. Once outside the caves, you can walk up Jacob's Ladder to the top of the gorge; the views are amazing, but it's quite a trek – 274 steps if we counted right. No wonder they're seeking planning permission to build a cable car, which they hope will do the same trip in a more leisurely way. The look-out tower up at the top has views of the Somerset Levels and Glastonbury Tor, and a very satisfying trail takes you some three miles around the gorge. Also included in the ticket (between March and October) is a tour bus through some of the narrow roads of the gorge, with a decent commentary, but don't let that stop you exploring at least a little of the area yourself on foot. You can arrange introductory sessions of caving, climbing and abseiling for children over 11 (you have to book in advance, and there are height restrictions). On summer evenings between 8 and 10 the whole area is distinctively lit with coloured lights. Meals, snacks, unusual shops; cl 24–25 Dec; (01934) 742343; £7.90 adults, £5 children 5–15. The family ticket, covering two adults and two children, is £21.50.

In Cheddar itself, children are welcome for the enjoyable food at the 16th-c Gardeners Arms (Silver St).

31. Tropiquaria

(A39, Washford – easy to spot by tall radio masts) This enjoyable place is an amazing transformation of a 1930s BBC transmitting station into an indoor jungle with high waterfall, tropical plants, free-flying birds and weird and wonderful animals. You can touch all sorts of creatures: plenty of snakes and lizards, maybe a giant millipede. There's an aquarium beneath the hall, while out in the landscaped gardens are birds, lemurs, chipmunks, guinea-pigs and wallabies, as well as a couple of good play areas inc two recently added pirate adventure ships. A delightful puppet theatre (for many, the highlight) has 20-min marionette and shadow puppet shows (usually hourly in summer, but at other times much less frequently – so worth checking first). Also an intriguing collection of vintage radios and televisions. Meals, snacks, shop, disabled access (not to aquarium); open daily Easter–Oct, then wknds and school hols Nov, Feb and Mar; (01984) 640688; £4.95.

After lunch (our top recommendation in the area is the Notley Arms along the B3188 at Monksilver), you could visit the small working port at Watchet. Fishing boats and coasters use its tidal harbour, and there's enough industry to keep it from being too touristy – though it's by no means unattractive.

An alternative for older families would be Dunster, with much more to see – really worth a day in its own right. There are fine medieval houses along the wide main street below the wooded castle hill, as well as a handsome octagonal former yarn market and market cross, a lovely 15th-c priory church with particularly tuneful bells, and a well established doll museum in the Memorial Hall (cl Oct–Mar; small admission charge). If you plan to visit Exmoor the National Park Information Centre is a useful first stop. The Dunster Castle Hotel has decent food, and there's a wealth of tearooms. Dunster's highlights are:

Dunster Castle Dramatically set in a 28-acre park rich with exotic flora and even subtropical plants, the castle was largely rebuilt in the 19th c, but has older features inside such as the 17th-c oak staircase and gallery with its brightly painted wall hangings. Excellent views. Shop in 17th-c stables, disabled access (a buggy avoids the steep climb up the hill); castle cl Thurs, Fri, and early Nov–Mar (gardens open all year); (01643) 821314; £6, £3.50 garden and park only; NT.

Old Dovecot (St George's St) In summer you can go right up this 12th-c dovecote, special for still having its potence, or revolving ladder, used for harvesting the plump squabs from the nesting boxes.

Watermill Well restored 18th-c mill still grinding and selling flour; teas in a pleasant riverside garden. Cl Fri (exc Jul–Aug), and all Nov–Mar; (01643) 821759; *£2.20.

32. Animal park in a great estate

Cricket St Thomas Park (Cricket St Thomas) In the lovely parkland of a great estate (still remembered by fans of *To The Manor Born*), this wildlife centre with a good emphasis on conservation is home to over 600 animals, many endangered in the wild. A highlight is a walk through the lemur woods, where you can see the primates swinging happily from the trees above. There's plenty more to amuse children inc a pets corner, miniature railway and new crazy golf and safari jeep rides. Meals, snacks, shop, cl 25 Dec; (01460) 30111; £5.95.

33. Wings and walks

Fleet Air Arm Museum (Royal Naval Air Station, Yeovilton, off A359) Big place concentrating on the story of aviation at sea from 1908, and the history of the Royal Naval Air Service. Lively displays on the WRENS, the Falklands and Gulf Wars, jets and helicopters, as well as nearly 50 historic aircraft, and lots of models, paintings, weapons and photographs, plus an exhibition on supersonic flight.

A highlight is the carrier hall, which leads you through various parts of the aircraft carrier while it is involved in an assignment: lots of flashing lights and dialogue as you follow the tour of the bridge, the operations room and best (and noisiest) of all the flight deck. Viewing galleries look out over the aircraft using this busy base. Also adventure playground, and hi-tech flight simulator. You could easily spend a good few hours here. Meals, snacks, shop, disabled access; cl 24–26 Dec; (01935) 840565; £8.

The Kingsdon Inn at Kingsdon is the best nearby place for lunch.

Ham Hill Country Park (Stoke sub Hamdon) 140 acres of grassland and woodland, full of wildlife and plants. The hill has provided the stone for many of the villages in the area, producing that distinctive warm honey-coloured look. The elevated area of old stone quarries gives walkers splendid views; you can go E from here on paths past St Michael's Hill, topped by an 18th-c pepperpot tower, to Montacute.

34. Brownsea Island

In the middle of Poole's huge natural harbour, this unspoilt 500-acre island – reached by an enjoyable short ferry ride – is a splendid place to explore. If you like your attractions full of organised entertainments then it isn't for you, but if you prefer to take things at your own pace, and appreciate the idea of strolling across uncrowded beaches, heath and woodland, then you can have a delightfully memorable day out. Preserved by the National Trust, it's most famous as the site of the first scout camp in 1907. The best thing to do is simply wander around, which you can do very freely, except for around the castle, which isn't open to the public (it's owned by the John Lewis Group), and the nature reserve at the northern end. Run separately by the Dorset Wildlife Trust, this costs £2 extra (£1 for children 12–18) but is definitely worth a look, with self-guided tours in Apr, May, Jun and Sept, but guided walks only in July and Aug. The whole island is good for spotting red deer as well as having a neat little bird-watching hide, and a large heronry. There are three free walking trails you can pick up when you arrive at the pretty little buildings on the Quay; best for families are the one-hour Smugglers Trail, with activities for 6- to 10-year-olds, and the Explorers Trail, a simple map-reading challenge. Splendid views back to Poole, and, in good weather, across to the Isle of Wight; the best are from nr the top of the steps to the SE beach. The visitor centre has a video, and in summer holidays activities like painting, tree-measuring and clay making. Occasional special events for children: last year at Easter they had a dinosaur trail. In summer there's an open-air theatre with Shakespeare or opera; tickets go fast, so apply well in advance; (01202) 251987. It's easy to spend most of an undemanding day here – but make sure you check the time of the last ferry back. Ferries go from Poole Harbour (twice hourly, takes around 20 minutes, £5 return fare for adults, £3.50 children), Sandbanks (twice hourly, takes 10 minutes, £3 return for adults, £2 children), Bournemouth Pier (three a day, takes 25 minutes, £6 return adults, £1 children), and, less often, from Swanage. The island has a decent restaurant and shop, and some disabled access; open Apr–early Oct; (01202) 707744; the landing fee (free to NT members) is £3.50 adults, £1.50 children 5–17. A family ticket is £8.50 for two adults and up to three children, or £5 for one adult and three children. Footpaths can be muddy at times. No dogs or bikes. There's a holiday cottage – the island's very quiet indeed after the last boat leaves.

35. A friendly farm with lots for children

Putlake Adventure Farm (Langton Matravers) Children are

encouraged to join in the lively activities at this friendly unspoilt farm; they can help hand-milk the cows, collect eggs from the chickens, or bottle-feed the lambs and goats. They do pony and tractor rides, and there are plenty of delightful small animals to fuss over; a more novel feature is the daily ferret racing. Plenty of things to play on, from miniature or full-sized tractors to scramble over, to an adventure playground and indoor play area. On wet days most of the attractions move under cover. Meals, snacks, indoor and outdoor picnic areas, shop (look out for the colourful sand art), disabled access; open daily Apr–Oct, plus maybe wknds in Nov, Dec and Mar, phone to check; (01929) 422917; £4 (£3 children).

Along at Worth Matravers, the idiosyncratic old Square & Compass has decent simple snacks, glorious views and interesting walks nearby. The rock pool at nearby Dancing Ledge is said to have been cut by a local schoolmaster.

36. Chimps, monkeys and a staggering rock cove

Monkey World (Wool; off A35 towards Bere Regis) As enjoyable as it is worthwhile, this enthusiastic rescue centre for apes and monkeys delights visitors of all ages. The centre looks after all kinds of primates that are gradually reintroduced to natural surroundings. As well as the biggest group of chimpanzees you'll see outside Africa, residents include ring-tailed and ruffed lemurs, barbary macaques, capuchins and woolly monkeys, orang-utans and gibbons, all roaming and climbing in decent-sized open enclosures. Keepers give useful talks, and you can see baby chimps playing in their nursery. A range of play areas includes a 15-stage obstacle course, plus a pets corner, mini motor-bikes, and jet boats – it's a very satisfying fine weather half-day out for families; special events most bank hols. Meals, snacks (and picnic area), shop, disabled access (a few steep paths); cl 25 Dec; (0800) 456600; £6.

Lulworth Cove (B3070 SW of Wareham) One of the great natural sights on the south coast, this is a gigantic scoop, with rock strata exposed and displaying all manner of rock types and contortions. This beauty spot, a magnet for summer visitors and geologists, has a classic mini-walk W along the cliffs to Durdle Door, a natural arch eroded by the sea; the unusually shaped rocks are surrounded by particularly good beaches. There are exhibitions on smuggling and country wines in the Lulworth Cove Heritage Centre (cl 24–25 Dec; nearby parking £2 for two hours).

The thatched Castle Inn (West Lulworth) is a popular food stop.

37. A day out in Weymouth

Deep Sea Adventure (Custom House Quay) Fascinating look at underwater exploration, shipwrecks, and the search for buried treasure, with lots of interactive displays. There's an exemplary exhibition on the *Titanic*, and a first-class indoor play area (£3 extra). Meals, snacks, shop, disabled access; cl 25–26 Dec and 1 Jan; (01305) 760690; £3.75.

Nothe Fort (Barrack Rd) Interesting armed Victorian fort on three levels, spread over a staggering 70 rooms. Children can clamber over some of the vehicles and guns, and there are fine views of the harbour and coast. Snacks, shop, some disabled access; open daily May–end Sept, Easter hols and Oct half-term, plus Sun pm and bank hols rest of year; (01305) 766626; £3.

Good views too from the garden of the Nothe Tavern (with tasty fresh fish), and from the pleasant nearby Nothe Gardens.

Weymouth itself has elegant 18th- and 19th-c terraces along its curving esplanade, and some older buildings in the narrower partly pedestrianised streets behind. The harbour is lively, with big ferries leaving from the outer quay, and the town's inner ring road running one-way around the inner harbour; the seafront Dorothy has decent cheap food. On the far side of the harbour the narrow streets of the old town are worth exploring; there's a Tudor House on Trinity St. The resort has a good beach, and lots of lively family attractions.

Brewers Quay In the heart of the Old Harbour, this is a skilful conversion of a harbourside Victorian brewery into shopping and leisure complex, with plenty of good year-round activities. Timewalk imaginatively re-creates scenes from the town's history, and an interactive gallery takes an interesting look at its brewing heritage (£4.25). There's also a craft market, ten-pin bowling, microbrewery, and lively hands-on science centre. Several places to eat, and good specialist shops, disabled access (exc to Timewalk); cl 25–27 Dec, and last two wks in Jan; (01305) 777622; free admission to centre.

Opposite, the lively Red Lion, with lots of tables outside, is also useful for something to eat.

38. Cavaliers, Roundheads and racing sheep

Torrington 1646 (South St car park, Torrington) This lively heritage centre brings to life one of the lesser-known battles of the English Civil War, fought here in February 1646. Four or five actors, all in period clothes, and rarely stepping out of character, work hard to get children involved. The scene-setting first part is a fairly traditional exhibition of Civil War history, where you can try on a helmet or find out from touch-screens whether you'd have been a Cavalier or Roundhead. A video shows a large-scale reconstruction of the battle by the Sealed Knot. Small groups are ushered in and told to imagine they're back in the 17th c; the guide disappears and is replaced by a 17th-c local keen to usher you away from the battle to safety. He'll take you through various reconstructions and situations, until you get to the church. Outside, army stragglers will try to sell you their armour and weapons; they'll show you how to charge into battle, let you examine their swords, and maybe introduce you to period games. Finally you're shown around a reconstructed 17th-c garden. Teas, snacks, picnic area, shop, disabled access; cl Sun and Mon outside school hols, and all mid-Dec to mid-Jan but best to check; (01805) 626146; £3.80, children £2.30. In this quiet dairy-farming town on a ridge above the River Torridge, the Black Horse (High St) is useful for lunch, and the Dartington Crystal glassworks (Linden Cl) has what's said to be Britain's biggest glass shop.

The Big Sheep (A39, 2m W of Bideford) Exuberant sheep centre, best known for its splendidly entertaining sheep steeple-chasing (usually around 3.20pm), when sheep with knitted jockeys on their backs race 200 yards from their field towards the prize of extra food. Even better are the duck trials half an hour later, miniature sheepdog trials with the sheep replaced by ducks; there are more traditional sheepdog demonstrations too. Other events and displays take in everything from shearing and bottle-feeding to milking, with plenty of opportunities to get close to the animals (lambs are born throughout the year, so always some to cuddle). Decent adventure play area, lots under cover, and it's good value – tickets are valid for unlimited return visits for a week for £1.50. Home-made meals and snacks (good teas), shop, disabled access; cl winter wkdys exc school hols (01237) 472366; £5.50.

The Thatched House family dining pub at Abbotsham is another lunch possibility.

39. Crealy Adventure Park

(Sidmouth Rd, Clyst St Mary) There's plenty to amuse children of all ages at this bustling family complex. The Magical Kingdom, a delightfully constructed area aimed mostly at under-7s, has play areas and a soaring gondola swing, while among the attractions to occupy older children are bumper boats, go-karts and a farm where you can milk the cows, and meet baby animals. Many of the attractions are indoors, inc some of the animals, and a very good varied adventure playground, with plenty of slides and things to swing on. Other attractions include a family roller-coaster, toddlers' garden play area, multicolour meadow, splash zone, pony rides and lakeside walks, and they have a particularly wide range of special events and activities (usually on summer Suns). Meals, snacks, shop, disabled access; (01395) 233200; cl Mon during term time Nov–Feb, 25–27 Dec and 1 Jan; £5.99; several family tickets available.

If you don't want to eat in the park, the Half Moon has decent food.

40. A day out in Exmouth

World of Country Life (Sandy Bay) 40 acres of decent family-based activities, with friendly animals, adventure playground and under-cover play areas, safari rides through deer and llama paddocks, reconstructed Victorian street, classic motorcycle collection, crafts, steam engines, and falconry centre. Meals, snacks, shop, disabled access; cl Nov–Easter; (01395) 274533; £5.75.

Exmouth is a good family seaside holiday town, well worth a visit for its lively harbour and marina, its long sandy beach and its stately church. Summer cruise trips go from the harbour up to Topsham, and there are sea fishing trips from the landing stage on the seafront (they supply rod and bait); (01395) 222144 for both. The Seafood Restaurant (Tower St) has nothing but the freshest fish and shellfish; the Grove (attractive seafront garden and play area) is useful too.

41. Boats, battlements and steam trains

River trips between Dartmouth and Totnes A good way of passing some of Devon's prettiest scenery, much of which can't be seen on foot or by car; you can combine this with steam trains or a connecting bus back – which saves hearing the commentary a second time. You can also go on circular tours of the surrounding area – known as doing a 'Round Robin'. There are some boats in winter – (01803) 834488 to check; £10.50 return to Totnes; (01364) 642338 for the South Devon Railway timetable.

Dartmouth Castle (slightly SE of town, off B3205) Classic late 15th-c battlemented fortress, virtually intact, with cannon and later gun batteries (a video display shows it firing), and great views out into the Channel. Snacks, shop; cl winter lunchtimes, and all day Mon and Tues Nov–Mar, also 24–26 Dec and 1 Jan; (01803) 833588; £3.20; EH. In summer a little ferry leaves the South Embankment for here every 15 mins or so. Otherwise it's an enjoyable and fairly gentle 20-min walk from Dartmouth itself, though the immediate hinterland is unremarkable.

Dartmouth is a charming waterside small town with many exceptional buildings, esp around the inner harbour. Though so popular, it's kept its own strong character, and stays very much alive through the winter. Cobbled Bayards Cove, with old fort and steep wooded hills behind, is particularly photogenic, as is pedestrianised Foss St. Markets Tues, Fri: Old Market is picturesque. Interesting shops, plenty of waterside seats, lots of action on the river. Parking in summer can be trying: best to use good park-and-ride on B3207 Halwell Rd.

Café Alf Resco (Lower Rd) is a bustling popular food place, and the cheerful Carved Angel Café (Foss St) does more imaginative food.

42. Woodland Leisure Park

(off A3122, Blackawton) For children who like to charge around and let off steam, this is one of the best days out in Devon. The emphasis is firmly on fairly traditional family fun – no major surprises or hugely elaborate rides, but good value activities and entertainment that somehow seem far more enjoyable; children up to around 12 can spin out a visit here for most of the day. A highlight for children at the upper end of the age range is the Twister, an exhilarating spiralling and plunging water-coaster – be prepared to get wet; there are several similar waterchutes nearby, and a very exciting toboggan run, the Tornado. Younger children enjoy the small zoo with wallabies, llamas and foreign and exotic birds (this year they added some particularly menacing-looking vultures), and there are stacks of well thought out play areas ranging from a commando-style assault course to imaginative under-cover areas for toddlers, with plenty of slides, ball pools, swinging tyres and rope bridges. They now have five floors of rides and activities indoors, including a ferris wheel, and the chance to drop well over 10 metres (40 ft) to experience weightlessness, so though you'll get the most out of a visit here in dry weather, it's still a good bet when the sun's sulking. Younger children are looked after particularly well: there's a nicely put-together Wild West town aimed at the under-5s, with miniature bellows in the forge, and a slide down from the mine. Also a honey farm with millions of bees behind glass, as well as a tractor yard, paddling pool, pedal karts and twice daily falconry displays. Particularly good activities around Hallowe'en, Bonfire Night, and wknds up to Christmas, and in school holidays you'll usually find face painting, and a clown or a juggler. It's the kind of place that adults enjoy vicariously, though there are boats on the lake, and plenty of quieter areas for woodland walks (and if Dad manages to slip off leaving Mum in charge, or vice versa, both the George and the Normandy Arms in the village are good pubs). They don't allow dogs, but do provide kennels; and they have an adjacent caravan park. Meals, snacks, shop, disabled access; cl Nov–mid-Mar exc wknds and school hols; (01803) 712598; £6.10 adults and children – a family ticket for two adults and two children is £22.95. It costs less in winter, when the water rides aren't open.

43. A hotch-potch of animal fun

Butterfly Park & Dartmoor Otter Sanctuary (Dart Bridge Rd, Buckfastleigh) You can watch otters swimming and playing from an underwater viewing tunnel, or see them on land in the six big landscaped enclosures; summer feeding times (readers enjoy this part most) 11.30, 2 and 4.30. Also under-cover tropical garden with free-flying butterflies and moths. Meals, snacks, shop, disabled access; cl Nov– Feb; (01364) 642916; £4.95. Combined with a trip on the South Devon Railway (the trains stop here), this makes for a very pleasant day out.

    Pennywell (Lower Dean, off A38 just S of Buckfastleigh) Friendly and unfussy, with over 750 animals in 80 acres, as well as lovely scenery, wildlife viewing hides, and barn owl demonstrations. Different events every half hour, from milking and feeding to ferret racing and worm charming, so always something for children to get involved in; also play areas, an assault course, go-kart ride, theatre, pony and donkey rides and an area where children can try out crafts like basket weaving. Meals, snacks, shop, disabled access; open wknds in Nov and Feb (phone for Christmas opening), Feb half-term, then daily late Mar–Oct; (01364) 642023; £5.95.

    The Dartbridge Inn (Totnes Rd) is a big bustling place with good value family food, and the more homely White Hart (Plymouth Rd) has some toys as well as good home cooking, with barbecues on some summer weekends in its pretty courtyard.

44. Morwellham Quay

Thriving and meticulously researched open-air museum in lovely countryside, with costumed guides convincingly re-creating the boom years when Morwellham was the greatest copper port in the Empire. You can watch the work of a cooper, assayer, coachmen and quay workers. Very popular in school hols – a visit can easily last all day. Meals, snacks, shop, disabled access limited but reduced price admission; cl Christmas wk; (01822) 832766; £8.90 (reduced price and operations in winter). The Ship (part of the centre) is a good place for a bite to eat, with period waitresses and drinks.

45. A day out in Plymouth

National Marine Aquarium (Barbican) The hundreds of fish at this excellent aquarium are shown in elaborate reconstructions of their natural habitats, starting with a moorland stream and bog, and progressing over the three floors through an estuary, seashore, and coral reef. Plenty of sound and other effects make the environments as authentic as possible – there's even a moorland mist rolling down the tor side. Most impressive of all is the huge two-storey-deep reef tank, designed to represent the deeper offshore waters around the British Isles, and containing over half a million litres of water. Divers descend into the depths to feed the fish by hand at various times. Also discovery pools for children, and Europe's largest collection of seahorses. The Shark Theatre has spooky lighting to create an appropriate air of menace. They usually feed the sharks Mon, Weds and Fri – check in advance to make sure. Restaurant with nice views over Plymouth Sound, shop, disabled access; cl 25 Dec; (01752) 220084; £6.75 (£4 children 4–15; good value family ticket, £19). Tickets usually allow same day re-entry.

    Crownhill Fort (Crownhill Fort Rd, just N) The biggest and least altered of Plymouth's Victorian forts, though from the road it looks little more than a wooded hill. Used by the army right up to 1986, it's been well restored by the Landmark Trust, with barrack rooms, underground tunnels, secret passageways, and lookout towers to explore; children can run around quite freely, and there's an adventure playground. You can stay here in a Victorian officer's flat (all year), and have the run of the place after dark. Snacks, shop, limited disabled access (lots of steep steps); cl Nov–Mar; (01752) 793754; £3.75.

The Barbican Carefully restored since the war, a series of narrow twisty streets of old buildings W of working Sutton Harbour; photogenic – and evocative even in wet weather. New St is its oldest core. The Dolphin pub has original Beryl Cook paintings, and the Notte (Notte St) has enjoyable food. In places the Hoe has something of the feel of smaller seaside promenades, with great views out over the Sound; decent food from the Yard Arm (looking out in suitably nautical style) and the Waterfront bar/restaurant.

46. Seaside monkey business (Looe)

Monkey Sanctuary (signed off B3253 at No Man's Land, just E of Looe) A fascinating place this; established in 1964, its wooded grounds are home to a colony of amazonian woolly monkeys. All were born here, and talks by staff give an intriguing insight into the dynamics and politics of the monkey community. Meals, snacks, shop, disabled access; cl Fri, Sat, and Oct–wk before Easter; (01503) 262532; *£4.

Looe itself is a seaside resort packed with tourist shops, teashops and pubs, but with a nice easy-going atmosphere even in high season. The old fishing village with its picturesque harbour and narrow little back streets is now immersed in tourism, and is the main shark-fishing place (on 'shark-fishing' trips you watch others doing the catching). From the quay there are summer **boat trips**, the easiest out to nearby St George's Island.

The Olde Salutation (Fore St) has good simple food and plenty of atmosphere, though the family room is fairly plain; the Smugglers

(Middle Market St) has a decent friendly restaurant, and the Trawlers (The Quay) has very good unusual seafood.

47. Eden Project

(well signed E of St Austell) Interest in this mammoth £86 million project was so great that half a million visitors came during 2000 just to see it being built. It's now fully opened, if not completely finished: several features are likely to grow over the next few years. Originally intended to be the world's largest greenhouse, it's like a space-age version of Kew Gardens, focusing on how plants from around the world affect us all, with enough unexpected features to stop it seeming worthy or dull, and a design that rarely fails to impress visitors of all ages. The 35-acre site is a conversion of an old china-clay pit: you start in a visitor centre perched on the edge of the pit, from where you'll have your first view of the place's most dramatic features, the huge conservatories (called biomes) that look like domes made from a silvery bubblewrap designed for an alien landscape. Constructed with massive hexagonal panels that slot together like a giant Meccano set, these are amazing to walk through, particularly the bigger Humid Tropics Biome, which effortlessly fits in a re-created rain forest, lagoon and 25-metre waterfall, with all the plants you'd expect to find in that kind of environment (and maybe some birds and insects too). The colourful Warm Temperate Biome features plants from the Mediterranean and California, while outside are developing gardens showcasing what you'd find in a temperate climate like that of Britain, or the Himalayas. But this isn't simply a glorified garden centre: the displays explain how people live in various climates, and how plants are used for food, medicine, and to make everything from tyres to toothpaste and trainers. They've worked hard to make it interesting: instead of putting all the information on boards and things to read, the points are made rather more inventively with art, sculpture, or music – perhaps pigs carved from wood, a live band, or a big sampling of teas from around the world. Adventure trails have hands-on activities and workshops for children: don't expect elaborate play areas or computer displays (though it can be fun, this isn't a theme park), but there's plenty to keep lively minds amused for half a day or more; at times it really feels as if you're wandering into different parts of the world. What impresses most is the staff – friendly and always ready to explain things in an accessible and interesting way. It's a joy in winter, but the Humid Tropics biome can feel very warm at other times, so don't wear your chunkiest jumper in this part: there's an air-conditioned cabin tucked amongst the trees if it gets too much. Lots of appealingly diverse places to eat (everything from great noodles to a proper Cornish pasty), good shops, disabled access; cl 24–25 Dec; (01726) 811911; *£9.50 adults, £4 children 5–15. The family ticket is good value at £22, covering entry for two adults and up to three children. You can usually buy fast track tickets from St Austell Tourist Information Centre; they won't save money, but should save time queuing at the entrance.

A strongly contrasting place for lunch is the Rashleigh at Polkerris, looking across St Austell Bay from its isolated beach, with a well restored ancient stone quay.

48. King Arthur and a dramatic castle

King Arthur's Great Halls (Fore St, Tintagel) Far from being a light-hearted romp, Arthurian legends are treated very earnestly here, and there's no denying the impressive craftsmanship, esp in the 72 stained-glass scenes. The best bit though is the tour's light show, which is narrated by Robert Power and gives the outline of the legend. Decent shop, disabled access; cl 25 Dec, limited opening hours in winter; (01840) 770526; £2.75.

Tintagel Castle Forgetting the myths and legends, these dramatic 12th- and 13th-c ruins have a spectacular setting and unrivalled views. A good start is from Rocky Valley, a craggy valley leading from the B3263 to the sea. Try to come out of season, when the crowds are fewer and the mist and crashing waves add a touch of mystery. There's quite a lot of climbing involved, and the often steep steps among the crags can be slippery in wet weather. Shop; cl 24–26 Dec and 1 Jan; (01840) 770328; £3; EH. In summer, a Land Rover can ferry you to the site from the village (a tourist trap since the 19th c) at regular intervals throughout the day. The Old Malthouse is a useful food stop, doing cream teas as well as lunches, and the parish **church** is worth a look.

49. Country crafts, and horses big and small

Shires (Tredinnick, just S of St Issey) Far more to this busy complex than just the magnificent shire horses which give its name: there's a children's farm, an exhibition of rural antiquities, nature trails, watermill and working craftsmen, and very big indoor and outdoor adventure playgrounds inc animated animal shows. The horses are displayed in an indoor arena, and you can see them being groomed in their stables – along with shetland ponies. Lots for all ages, but ideal for children. Meals, snacks, shop, disabled access; cl Nov–Easter; (01841) 540276; £6.

The Ring o' Bells in St Issey does good home cooking, and a little way off the Quarryman at Edmonton also has good food, with a distant view of a big wind farm.

50. Seals, ships and a castle

National Seal Sanctuary (Gweek) Britain's largest marine mammal rescue centre, the National Seal Sanctuary provides a home for dozens of injured or orphaned seals that they hope to be able to release back into the wild, all with their own names and character traits. Underwater observatories, feeding-time fun, woodland walks, play area, as well as donkeys, ponies and goats, an audio-visual display and a nature trail. A new sea lion pool should be open by the time this book comes out. Snacks and summer barbecues, shop, disabled access; cl 25 Dec; (01326) 221361; £6.50. The Gweek Inn is a handy nearby family pub, and the Trengilly Wartha at Nancenoy is excellent for lunch, with a nice walk down to Scotts Quay on the creek.

Pendennis Castle (1m SE of Falmouth) Superb views from this well preserved fort, one of Henry VIII's chain of coastal defences; displays of firearms and uniforms in the museum, a hands-on discovery centre and World War II guardroom with cells. Snacks, shop, some disabled access; cl 24–26 Dec, 1 Jan; £3.80; EH.

Falmouth, the county's biggest town, has a huge natural harbour full of sailing boats of every description, big sea-going ships, little passenger ferries (to St Mawes and Truro – great fun) and boat trips (2-hr trip £5.50; (01326) 374241); they also now have a summer road train that stops at all the town's main attractions (£4.25 for an all-day ticket). It's also a busy but pleasant shopping centre, with some nice old-fashioned streets, ships' chandlers and a good bustling atmosphere, though surprisingly few sea views. Broad avenues of spiky-leaved dracaena trees away from the centre give it quite a foreign feel.

The Quayside and Chain Locker by the inner harbour do useful food, and the Warehouse is an enjoyable waterside restaurant.

51. Parrots and pottering

Paradise Park (Hayle) The World Parrot Trust's HQ, with some of the beautiful and sometimes rare residents shown to spectacular effect in the huge Parrot Jungle, a splendid mix of waterfalls, swamps and streams. You can try feeding lorikeets in the Australian aviary (nectar for sale in the shop), and there are lots of other exotic birds and numerous animals, inc miniature horses, pygmy goats and red pandas, some of which you can feed at the Fun Farm. Daily free-flying bird show (usually at 12.30), summer bird of prey displays (not Sat exc July–Aug), entertaining penguin and otter feeding shows, children's quiz trails, big play area, and a narrow-gauge railway gently rattling through the park. Adults may prefer the Victorian walled garden (lovely clematis arches in May) or the pub that brews its own real ale. Not just for exotic creatures, the park has initiated a scheme to reintroduce the rare chough to its native countryside, after an absence of 26 years, and you can also see red squirrels. Meals, snacks, shop (and plant sales), mostly disabled access; (01736) 751020; £6.50 (£3.95 children over 4), usually with return.

St Ives A pretty place, despite the summer crowds, with its attractive working harbour and narrow streets and alleys (the cobbled Fore St is the prettiest). It has good wide beaches, and plenty of bird life along the Lelant Saltings (RSPB reserve). The waterside Sloop (interesting pictures for sale) is reliable for lunch, and the recently reworked Pedn Olva overlooking Porthminster beach has enjoyable modern food. The surfers' favourite beach is Porthmeor slightly N, while in the other direction the B3306 to Land's End has great coast and moorland views. Out of season, when the caravan and camp sites are empty, the magnificent sands around St Ives Bay are well worth walking, with good cliff walks to the west.

52. Land's End

The most westerly point of England, with wild and blustery walks along dramatic clifftops, and on a clear day views out as far even as the Isles of Scilly. The 200-acre site has been extensively developed for families over the years, and it's become almost like a theme park, with 'multi-sensory experiences', gift shops, craft centres, farm animals, burger bars and plenty to amuse children. The exhibitions and hi-tech displays are a useful enough introduction to the folklore of the area, there's also a Wildlife Trust hut, and an RSPB observation hide has information on the coastline's wildlife. Meals, snacks, shopping arcade, good disabled access; cl 24–25 Dec; (01736) 871501; £9 for all attractions, less off-season. A public right of way goes through here to Land's End itself, so you're not obliged to buy a ticket if you just want to walk to the end of England. The same goes for the fine cliff walks in both directions – the one to Sennen is lovely, and the cove there is worth looking around, with the Old Success an enjoyable place for family lunches. Some of the wildest and most formidable cliffs in Britain are between here and Treen.

Northern England & North Wales

Including North Wales, Cheshire, County Durham, Cumbria, Derbyshire, Lancashire, Lincolnshire, Northumberland, Nottinghamshire, the northern part of Shropshire, Staffordshire and Yorkshire.

SEE MAP 3

1. Steam trains, owls and a splendidly unstuffy stately home

Muncaster Castle & Owl Centre (A595, 1m E of Ravenglass) The same family have lived in the elegant house since 1208, and will continue to do so as long as a magical glass drinking bowl remains intact. Extended over the centuries (esp the 19th) from its original tower, it still feels very lived-in, and the rich furnishings and décor include some fine Elizabethan furniture and embroidery. There's an entertaining Walkman tour, and young children will especially like the underground maze (you can advance only by answering questions about the environment). Muncaster is the HQ of the World Owl Trust, and they have over 180 birds from 50 different species; an interpretation centre has closed circuit TV of nesting owls. There are talks and flying displays at 2.30pm, and you can watch wild herons being fed (every afternoon Mar–Nov, weather permitting). The lovely 77-acre grounds are particularly rich in species rhododendrons and have unusual trees, nature trails, adventure play area and lots of rescued birds of prey. Various special events. Meals, snacks, shops, good plant centre, mostly disabled access; house open pm daily (exc Sat) from 12 Mar to 5 Nov, garden and owl centre open all year; (01229) 717614; £6.50 for everything, £5 for the garden, owl centre and maze.

Ravenglass & Eskdale Railway England's oldest narrow-gauge steam trains, lovingly preserved, with open carriages chugging up seven miles of unspoilt valley to Dalegarth; admirers say it's the most beautiful train journey in England. Cafés each end, and a small museum (free) at Ravenglass. Shop, disabled access (with notice); cl most of Nov–Mar, but best to phone for train times and dates; (01229) 717171; £7 return. Enjoyable 3-hr summer walk back from Boot (walks booklets from stations). Up at Boot, the Burnmoor Inn does good family lunches, and has a fine play area. There are guided tours of Eskdale Watermill, an attractively set working 16th-c oatmeal mill nearby, with a picnic area nr woodland waterfalls. Snacks, shop; cl Mon and all Oct–Mar; (019467) 23335; £1.25.

2. South Lakes Wild Animal Park

(Crossgates, N of Dalton-in-Furness) Very committed, rapidly expanding wildlife centre, well placed for fine views of the entire Furness peninsula. A particular highlight is watching their Sumatran and Amur tigers clamber up a 20-ft vertical pole to hunt their meat (daily at 2.30). Also fun is the chance to hand-feed their big collection of kangaroos, the only place you can do this outside Australia. Gathered together according to the continents they hail from, residents include rhinos, zebra, giraffe and cheetahs, with lots of smaller creatures such as meerkats, pandas, coatis and porcupines. A four-acre section has wallabies and emus waiting to be fed; play area, and a miniature railway (Apr–Sept). Snacks, shop, disabled access; cl 25 Dec; (01229) 466086; £7 (£4 children 3–15). Admission is half-price Nov–Feb.

The nearby Black Dog is a friendly country pub with hearty home cooking. Dalton itself has a rather austere square castle.

3. Lakeland Wildlife Oasis

(Hale, A6 S of Milnthorpe) Millions of years of evolution flash before your eyes at this lively jungle house, a fascinating cross between zoo and museum. Interactive displays alongside the brightly coloured and unusual fish, birds, insects and animals, and woodland where children can crawl along tunnels overlooking the meerkat enclosure. Activities include fossil rubbing and an animal rubber-stamping trail. Snacks, shop, disabled access; cl 25–26 Dec; (015395) 63027; £5.50. The B5282 to Arnside has quiet estuary and mountain views, and the road leads on up to Silverdale (actually just over the Lancashire boundary), a little-visited peaceful oasis. This hilly countryside is well suited both to walkers and to drivers, and the coastline is particularly interesting to bird-watchers and naturalists. The small town looks out over the tidal sands to the Cumbrian hills, with streets of quiet houses and a church that looks 14th-c but was built barely a century ago. Various crafts are sold at the Georgian buildings of the Wolf House Gallery (Gibraltar), so named because a former occupant of the house was reputed to have killed the last wolf in England. It also has an adventure playground and a courtyard garden; good new café, some disabled access (with notice); cl Mon Apr–Dec, and all wkdys Jan–Mar; (01524) 701405; free. There are good woodland walks behind the town, readers recommend the Waterslack tearooms (past the station), and the Silverdale Hotel on Shore Rd is worth knowing.

Leighton Moss Nature Reserve (off Yealand Redmayne Rd) RSPB reserve with several roomy hides looking out on to reedbeds where bitterns, bearded tits and marsh harriers breed;

good walks and views and a recently refurbished visitor centre. Events and guided walks throughout the year. Meals, snacks, shop, disabled access; cl 25 Dec; (01524) 701601; £4.50 (RSPB members free). The Moss is also crossed by a (free) public footpath.

4. A day out in Penrith

Rheged Discovery Centre (Redhills) Named after the Celtic kingdom which once stretched from Strathclyde to Cheshire, this vast development – Europe's largest grass-covered building – is set right into a hillside, and pays homage to all things Cumbrian. The history of the county is brought to life on a cinema screen the size of six double-decker buses, and a separate video display takes a look at contemporary life through the eyes of six local people. There's a hands-on exhibition devoted to the history of mountaineering, plus changing exhibitions of local art (some of it for sale), an in-house potter, workshops, specialist shops and restaurants promoting local produce. The huge glass atrium gives views across to the High Pennines. Meals, snacks, shop, disabled access; (01768) 868000; cinema £4.95.

    Wetheriggs Pottery (Clifton Dykes, signed off A6 S) Interesting and very smart working pottery – one of the oldest in the country – with 19th-c steam engine and equipment; children can try their hands at the wheel, and there's a play area and birds of prey. Restaurant, shop, disabled access; cl Tues, plus Weds Sept–Easter, 25–26 Dec, and 1 Jan; (01768) 892733; free (exc Aug, £2.50).

    Penrith Castle Built in the 14th c as a defence against Scottish raids, and the home of Richard III when he was Duke of Gloucester. The ruins are surrounded by a park; free.

    A real locals' rather than tourists' town, and the biggest in Lakeland, Penrith is very much a northern country town with solid stone streets and genuinely traditional Lakeland shops. The Museum on

Middlegate is a useful introduction to the area, and the George does decent lunches.

5. Friendly animals and a glorious lake

Trotters World of Animals (Coalbeck Farm, nr Bassenthwaite Lake, signed from A591 and A66 as Trotters and Friends) Everything you'd expect from a friendly farm, but a few surprises too: you're as likely to see a golden eagle or boa constrictor as you are sheep and cows. The range of animals at this 25-acre site really is wide, from rare breeds of pigs, cattle and goats, through birds of prey, lizards and snakes, to otters, llamas and gibbons. Most of them are seen fairly close up: throughout the day, at certain times, you might be able to bottle-feed a baby goat, cuddle the rabbits, or have a hawk fly down to your wrist. There's usually something happening every half hour, so it's not too hard to stretch a visit to half a day or more. Quite a few things are under cover, so although like most farms it's best in dry weather, don't rule it out if it looks like rain. In winter they keep up a full range of indoor activities, and Father Christmas generally pops in too. For an extra charge they usually have trailer rides or pony rides. There's a decent presence of helpful uniformed staff on hand to answer questions, an adventure playground, and plenty of space for a picnic. No dogs. Their birds of prey centre has the region's only breeding golden eagles and caracaras. Meals, snacks, shop (they sell feed for some of the animals), disabled access; cl winter wkdys, and 25 Dec, 1 Jan; (017687) 76239; *£4.50 adults, £2.75 children 3–14.

If there's still some energy to expend, drive back through Keswick and out on the B5289 along **Derwent Water**. The lake looks magnificent from walks up Friar's Crag by the waterside, just outside Keswick) from Castlehead Wood (also just S of Keswick), and from Walla Crag (a more adventurous climb from the NT car park at Great

Wood, an area teeming with red squirrels). Or you can hire rowing boats and launches in the town (017687) 72263. Regular launches run all year from Keswick to half a dozen points around the lake.

The Dog & Gun (Lake Rd) is our current pick of the Keswick pubs for good value family lunches.

6. Animal fun, and an eco-friendly eye-opener

Whitehouse Farm Centre (2m N of Stannington, towards Tranwell) Bustling place with a good variety of animals from chinchillas, snakes and mice to llamas, 15 different breeds of sheep and a shire horse. In an under-cover area, children can touch lots of the smaller animals (often piglets, lambs and other baby animals here). Also soft play area, adventure playground, pedal tractors (50p for proper tractor rides), and activities such as candle-making and face-painting. A few craft stalls inc a blacksmith, candle-maker and embroiderer. Meals, snacks, shop, disabled access; cl Mon in term-time, wkdys Nov and Jan; (01670) 789998; £3.25.

The Ridley Arms in Stannington has good value food all day.

Earth Balance (Bomarsund; signposted off A189 N of Bedlington) Enjoyable place spread over 260 acres, showcasing environmentally friendly living, with organic food and drink made on the premises, a green garden centre, and Re-Dress, where new clothes and textiles are made out of recycled products. A trail takes you around eco-buildings, a willow maze, a nature reserve, and a fishing lake that provides power for the complex. Readers enjoy the Cat & Sawdust pub here, with ales brewed in the site's solar-powered brewery, and there's a good choice of locally made food and crafts in the café and shop. Disabled access is difficult in some parts of the trail; cl 23 Dec–2 Jan; (01670) 821000; free.

7. From Hadrian's Wall to DNA in Newcastle

There's enough here to fill two busy days, without even exploring the lively places along the Tyne – pick and choose for a treat of a day out.

Segedunum (Buddle St/Station Rd, Wallsend) A lot bigger than any of the other museums along Hadrian's Wall, this has well put together new displays giving an excellent idea of everyday life in Segedunum, the fort that once stood here, and take an intriguing look at how the site developed over the centuries that followed. The remains of this great terminal fort lay buried under Victorian housing until the 1970s, after which they were excavated more thoroughly than just about any other site in the Empire: you can see plenty of the finds. The most striking feature of the complex is the spectacular 35-metre (115-ft) viewing tower, which super-imposes virtual reality reconstructions on the actual excavations. Another unique feature is a completely functional reconstructed Roman bathhouse. Elsewhere are videos, more reconstructions, and plenty of hands-on and touch-screen activities, many at child's height. There are also galleries on mining (there was once a colliery here) and shipbuilding (Swan Hunter are based next door). Children under 6 aren't going to be engaged for long, but older ones can be happily distracted for an hour or two, particularly if they learned about the Romans at school. Snacks, shop, disabled access; cl 25–26 Dec, 1 Jan; (0191) 295 5757; £2.95.

Discovery Museum (Blandford Sq) Thriving complex with galleries and interactive features on subjects likely to appeal to the whole family – it's the biggest and busiest museum in the area. A highlight is the interactive Science Factory with plenty to push, press and poke: TV effects create the illusion of flying down the Tyne, there's a soft play area for very young children, and lots of mirrors, magnets and microscopes to fiddle with. Other galleries offer a similarly hands-on look at the history of the city (inc the early days of Newcastle United), fashion, shipbuilding, army life, and local inventors. A newly refurbished multimedia gallery houses the remarkable 30-metre (100-ft) *Turbinia*, once the fastest ship afloat. They run family fun days every Sun, and during the Easter and summer hols. Snacks, shop, disabled access; cl Sun am, Good Fri, 25–26 Dec, 1 Jan; (0191) 232 6789; free.

Life Interactive World (Times Sq) In a dramatic building beside the city's main railway station, this innovative visitor centre explores the origins of life. You'd think anywhere setting out to explain DNA in an accessible way would be on to a loser, but the main exhibition areas put across serious science in a surprisingly entertaining way. A visit starts with the River of Life, a trip back through billions of years of evolution, tracing how mankind has got to where we are today. One highlight is the Crazy Motion, a simulator ride designed to make you feel you're surfing, roller-blading, and even bungee-jumping, and among numerous other interactive attractions is the chance to score against a virtual goalie. A live show in the Secret of Life explains what we have in common with everything from dinosaurs to daffodils, and a multi-media spectacle (shown in a theatre resembling a giant brain) aims to illustrate the range of emotions and activities going on in our heads. Meals, snacks, shop, disabled access; cl 25 Dec and 1 Jan; (0191) 243 8223; £6.95.

Laing Art Gallery (New Bridge St) Notable temporary exhibitions, and excellent children's gallery, the activities well designed to encourage young children to think about shapes, texture and patterns. Free guided tours of the main galleries 11.30 Sat. Meals, snacks, shop, disabled access; cl Sun am, Good Fri, 25–26 Dec, and 1 Jan; (0191) 232 7734; free.

8. North of England Open-Air Museum

(Beamish, A693) For many people this is the most rewarding paid attraction in Britain, an amazingly ambitious 300-acre museum exhaustively re-creating life in the North of England at the turn of the century. There are five main sections: a town with streets, shops, houses and businesses, a colliery village with mine, chapel, cottages and school, a manor house with formal gardens and orchard, a railway station, and a home farm with animals and craft demonstrations (ducks and geese wander around for extra authenticity). The buildings aren't just empty shells: costumed staff really bring the place to life, answering questions and showing off period crafts and skills. What's nice for children is that they really can get a feel for what life was like in the past; they can wander around touching everything and joining in most of the activities – learning how to play hoops and hopscotch for example, or taking part in lessons in the schoolroom (bad handwriting is rewarded by a light rap on the knuckles). Both the sweet factory and the dentist offer demonstrations, and a Victorian fairground has rides and a proper Hall of Mirrors (the only bit that has a small extra charge). A re-created engine shed has a magnificent 1822 locomotive, and a full-scale replica of Stephenson's Locomotion No. 1, which carries visitors down a ¼-mile track. There are extra activities most wknds, from vintage car rallies to Meccano-building, military re-enactments or whippet racing. In summer you may also find brass bands in the park, or choirs in the chapel. Working trams and buses link the different areas, and there's plenty of open space for picnics, or just to run around. No detail is overlooked, with something for everyone – though perhaps it's best on a dry day. Dogs are allowed on a lead. Meals and snacks (some in a period pub), good shops, some disabled access; cl Mon and Fri Nov–Mar, and Dec 10–Jan 1; (01913) 704000; £12 adults, £6 children. It's only £4 in winter, when only the town and tramway are open; the plus side of visiting then is that as there are fewer people, the guides can take more time to explain things.

The Shepherd & Shepherdess not far from the gate is useful for lunch, with glass-fibre monsters in its play area.

9. Dazzle and delight in Sunderland

National Glass Centre (Liberty Way, Sunderland) This dazzling place is a fascinating cross between gallery, museum and factory visit. In a striking glass structure on a sloping site alongside the River Wear (you can walk along the glass roof, looking down on the exhibitions below), it focuses on how glass is made and used all around the world. You can watch glass-blowing demonstrations. The Kaleidoscope Gallery explores the more imaginative ways glass is used, from time-lapse photography to a hall of mirrors. Several exhibits are interactive, with computer displays, and there's a changing exhibition programme. Meals, snacks, good shop, disabled access; cl 25 Dec, 1 Jan; (0191) 515 5555; £5.

Mowbray Park This redeveloping Victorian park has a children's play area with giant chess pieces, sculpture trail and swan house. Recently reopened after a £6 million refurbishment – there are now 11 galleries instead of 3 – the **Sunderland Museum and Art Gallery** takes a lively look at the town's history. Themes range from shipbuilding to archaeology and, not for the squeamish, in the natural history section you can find out about all the tiny creatures that live on our bodies and in our homes. Lots of interactive and hands-on displays; children can crawl down a mine shaft, touch fossils, and try on various old-fashioned clothes. One of the galleries is devoted to art, and contains quite a few works by Lowry, who often visited the town. Meals, snacks, shop, full disabled access; cl 25 Dec and 1 Jan; (0191) 5532323; free.

10. Historic Quay

At Hartlepool's old docks, this is a vivid open-air re-creation of an 18th-c port, complete with painstakingly reconstructed furnished houses, market, prison, and fully stocked shops. Also a couple of film shows, a dramatic (and noisy) exhibition on fighting ships, and the new maritime adventure centre with lots of fun activities: you can design your own tattoo, take a turn at rat-killing, and plot a ship's course using the stars. There's also a children's playship, and a virtual reality centre giving would-be sailors the chance to try life at sea without even getting wet. Lots to see, exceptionally well done. Meals, snacks, shop, disabled access; (01429) 860888; £5.50.

The stylish neighbouring Jacksons Landing is a good waterside factory shopping mall, with places to eat that include one done out as an 18th-c tavern.

11. The pick of Blackpool

Blackpool Pleasure Beach Founded in 1896, this is still one of Britain's most popular attractions. Altogether 145 rides and attractions are squeezed into the park's 42 acres, inc several roller-coasters that can whiz you through 360, backwards, or in the dark, their own Millennium Dome (a simulator here allows you to design your own fairground ride), bungee trampolines, ice-skating, and traditional rides such as ghost trains, River Caves, a Hall of Mirrors and dodgems. One of the best rides is the £15 million hi-tech water ride, Valhalla, full of drops and effects that include real fire. At six minutes, it's also currently the longest dark ride in the world, and you get very wet unless – for £1 extra – you hire one of their ponchos. There's still nothing to top the Big One though, a monster roller-coaster that climbs to 72 metres (235 ft) and reaches speeds of up to 85mph. Most of the more exciting rides have height restrictions but smaller children have their their own section of the park, which includes a fine miniature wooden roller-coaster, the Zipper Dipper. Meals and snacks (not just the expected fish and chips and takeaways), shops, disabled access (it's worth getting their detailed brochure in advance); open daily Easter–early Nov, plus wknds in Nov, Dec and Mar; (0870) 444 5566. Free entry to the park, then tickets for rides range from £1.30 to £2.30, or you can get a wristband offering unlimited rides on everything for £25 (£40 for two consecutive days). A child's wristband offering unlimited gentler rides is £10.95.

Blackpool Tower The outstanding landmark has several lively attractions geared towards families, inc a circus, laser shows, aquarium (rare giant sea turtles), science gallery, dinosaur dark ride, a lift to the top, and the Walk of Faith – a 5-cm-thick glass floor 116 metres (380 ft) above the ground. Perhaps most fun at night (they're open till 11pm in summer). You can try old-fashioned ballroom dancing, and there's non-stop cabaret music. Meals, snacks, shop, limited disabled access; cl winter wkdys (exc during Feb half-term); (01253) 622242; £10, more during the Illuminations, £5 after 8pm. These famous autumn light displays are the best of their kind, and they're continually adding new features – though you'll have to travel at a snail's pace along the Golden Five Hundred Yards (or Mile as they call it here) if you decide to drive.

Blackpool Zoo (East Park Drive) Over 400 animals in 32 acres of landscaped gardens inc a walk-through lemur wood, free-flying bird hall, and gorilla island. The big cats are usually fed at 3.30pm (not Fri), and the sea lions at 11am and 2.30pm; there are parrot displays at 11.45am and 2pm. Meals, snacks, shop, disabled access; cl 25 Dec; (01253) 830830; £6.50.

You can buy a Hopper Pass (£42) which allows you entrance to the Blackpool Tower, zoo, and Sandcastle leisure complex, and acts as a unlimited ride wristband at the Pleasure Beach.

12. Smuggling up-to-date – and very much more

Merseyside Maritime Museum (Albert Dock, Liverpool) Huge (and growing) museum spread over six floors, with boats, ships, craft demonstrations and a lively interpretation of what it was like for the millions who travelled from here to the New World. The Museum of Liverpool Life vividly re-creates social history from the last century or so, and the Customs and Excise museum, Anything To Declare, is much more fun than it sounds. It takes an intriguing look at concealment techniques, with demonstrations by sniffer dogs, and there's an interesting assortment of items seized by customs inc a guitar made from a turtle, a tiger-skin waistcoat, and a host of illegal weapons. A gallery on transatlantic slavery has divided local historians, who disagree on Liverpool's true role in the slave trade. Meals, snacks, shop, disabled access; cl 23–26 Dec, 1 Jan; (0151) 478 4499; free.

This whole Albert Dock area, a spectacular restoration of previously redundant warehouse buildings, is now a lively waterfront complex of shops, cafés and exhibitions, with regular entertainers, performers, events, boat trips and of course Fred's weather map. You can easily base a whole day around a visit here, with other major draws within the complex including the bouncy Beatles Story and (free) the Tate contemporary art gallery.

For a countryside alternative, head out to **Croxteth Hall & Country Park** (5m NE) Period displays in Edwardian house, and working farm, Victorian walled garden, miniature railway, and country walks in the grounds – a pleasant family trip out. Meals, snacks, shop, some disabled access; house cl Oct–Easter, farm cl 25 Dec–1 Jan, park open all year; (0151) 228 5311; park free, hall farm and garden £3.90, hall or farm only £1.95, walled garden only £1.15.

13. Camelot Adventure Theme Park

(Charnock Richard) One of the country's best and most imaginative theme parks, not least because they really have stuck with the Arthurian theme in just about all the well thought out entertainments. The spectacularly dizzying swing-boat ride is in the shape of Excalibur, the monorail round the place looks like a tamed dragon, and even the animals in their farm aren't out of place – they live in thatched and cobbled enclosures. A highlight is the splendid half-hour jousting display – twice a day in peak periods, but only once a day at the start and end of the season, so worth checking the time when you arrive; the seating is under cover. Dozens of other attractions include something for most age groups: older children are well catered for with thrill rides like the intriguingly designed Rack, the new looping Gauntlet, and the excellent dark roller-coaster Venom, but there are plenty of more sedate rides for younger visitors, with scaled-down roller-coasters to get them into the habit. You can bottle-feed lambs or help with milking at the farm, and there's a big indoor play area. Also log flume and other water rides, a magician and jester, and an odd new show with animatronic cats illustrating the life of a medieval knight. A couple of things have extra charges: the go-karts, and the driving school, where junior learners can get behind the wheel of a fire engine or a double-decker bus. There are perhaps a few too many arcade games, but otherwise this is the best place in the area for unadulterated fun: most children can happily spend a whole day here. It's best in dry weather, though a fair bit is under cover, and if it rains continuously for two hours you can get a half-price return ticket. You may find occasional special offers on their website, www.camelotthemepark.co.uk. Meals, snacks, shop, disabled access; open wknds and school hols Apr–Oct, daily Jun–Aug; (01257) 452100; £12 adults, and children over a metre (3 ft 3 in) tall – under that you get in free, but won't be allowed on some of the rides. The family ticket, £40 for two adults and two children, offers a good saving.

14. Wigan Pier

(Wallgate, Wigan) This dynamic and entertaining wharfside centre demonstrates local life in the early 1900s, with actors performing in a reconstructed mine, pub, school, music hall, houses and even seaside. An ingenious mix of museum and theatre, it's an enormously enjoyable family day out, and you really do get a tangible impression of what life was really like at the turn of the century. A museum takes a nostalgic look at each decade of the 20th c; you can see a Victorian schoolroom, mill steam engine and textile machinery hall, and take a canal boat trip. Meals, snacks, shop, disabled access; cl Fri (exc Good Fri), and 25–26 Dec; (01942) 323666; £6.95.

For a country contrast, **Haigh Hall Country Park** (N of Wigan) is a 250-acre country park with guided walks, nature trails, beautifully set golf course, craft centre, walled gardens, play area, crazy golf and miniature railway. Occasional tours of house – phone for dates, and a good programme of events. Meals, snacks, shops (one excellent for golfers), some disabled access; (01942) 832985; park free, charges for parking and attractions.

15. Machines, power, space – science in vivid action

Museum of Science & Industry (Castlefield, Manchester) One of Britain's most impressive and imaginative museums, built on the site of the oldest passenger railway station in the world. There are hours of things to do, and plenty to touch and fiddle with. The main galleries take a broad and accessible look at power, industry and transport (going right up to space travel), with highlights inc an exciting simulator in the air and space gallery, a big hands-on interactive science area, and a fascinating exhibition on sanitation. The vast power hall has working engines and railway locomotives, there's an absorbing exhibition on the history of photography, and a comprehensive look at Manchester's development. The changing exhibitions are particularly good – an exhibition on dinosaurs in the spring is followed by one on *Star Trek* that will run till Oct. Restaurant, shop, disabled access; cl 24–26 Dec (0161) 832 1830; free, charges for temporary exhibitions.

The nearby White Lion (Liverpool Rd) has good value food inc children's all day – and tables out among the excavated foundations of the Roman city, overlooking what was the fort gate. This whole area, by the basin where the Bridgewater and Rochdale canals meet, is interesting: restored warehouses, viaducts and the like, lots of lively redevelopment including a tramway and wonderfully light and airy footbridge, plenty going on, even street theatre, and a new visitor centre which should be open by the time this book comes out.

16. Birds, animals, a country walk and a historic house

Rockwater Bird Conservation Centre (Foxstones Lane, Cliviger – above Mereclough SE of Burnley) Expanding collection taking in waterfowl, pheasants, foreign birds and owls as well as rabbits and chipmunks. Children can feed some animals. Snacks, limited disabled access; cl Mon (exc bank hols), wkdys Mar and Oct, all Nov–Feb; (01282) 415016; £3.

Cliviger Gorge nearby has pleasant walks, with stream, woodland and farmland; moors above. The Kettledrum at Mereclough has good home cooking.

Towneley Hall (A646 S of Burnley) Home of the Towneley family from the 14th c until 1902; you can look around an Elizabethan long gallery, Regency rooms, and a Victorian kitchen.

The nearby art gallery has recently been refurbished, and there's a craft museum, natural history centre and aquarium. Woodland trails and space for picnics in the park. Shop, cl Sat, Sun pm, Christmas and New Year; free.

17. Cheese made interesting, and England's tallest waterfall

Hardraw Force (just N of Hawes at Hardraw) England's tallest waterfall cascading over a 30-metre (100-ft) lip; it's best after rain (though the paths can be muddy then), and at dry times you may see barely a trickle; small fee at Green Dragon pub. A longer excursion follows the Pennine Way from Hawes and over the River Ure. The valley above the falls is attractive, and this can be a start for a long day's walk to Great Shunner Fell.

Wensleydale Creamery (Gayle Lane, Hawes) You can watch the cheese being made by the traditional method, all by hand, and there's a fascinating visitor centre, with a well set out dairying/cheese museum. The shop (busy in summer) has samples of their variously flavoured cheeses – our favourite was the one with blueberries. Very good café, disabled facilities; cl 25 Dec; (01969) 667664; £2.

Dales Countryside Museum (Station Yard, Hawes) Interesting displays of local crafts and domestic and industrial life as well as hands-on exhibits, re-creations, a steam locomotive and displays on transport; also changing exhibitions and special events. Shop, disabled access; open daily Easter–end Oct, phone for winter opening times; (01969) 667450; *£3.

Hawes is busy in summer with hikers and coach-parties exploring Wensleydale, but pretty, and a proper market town, its Tuesday mart full of livestock in late summer. The Crown, Fountain and White Hart all do good value food, and there are several bric-a-brac shops worth poking around.

18. A high-spirited secret garden

Forbidden Corner (Tupgill Park Estate, Coverham) Enchantingly different, and really memorable: a labyrinth of tunnels, chambers, follies and surprises imaginatively laid out in an attractive four-acre walled garden. A clue-guide leads you over stepping stones, down dead ends, and through water walls to the centrepiece, an atmospheric underground grotto. Features include a huge glass pyramid, a 9-metre (30-ft) giant, optical illusions (a normal-looking corridor shrinks to a mere burrow), and statues that range from picnicking bears to griffins (watch out for the ones that squirt water). You can buy food to feed the mirror carp, and there are panoramic Coverdale views. Snacks, shop; open daily Apr–Oct, Sun Nov–23 Dec, phone to book; (01969) 640638; £5.

Coverdale is well worth exploring. Wensleydale's major tributary valley, it is fairly gentle in its lower reaches, but climbs high into a wild and untamed-feeling world of lonely sheep farms. Down in Middleham, both the Black Swan and the White Swan are good places for lunch.

19. Lightwater Valley Theme Park

(North Stainley) Family fun from the nostalgic pleasure of a steam train to the white-knuckle, green-faced thrills of one of the world's biggest roller-coasters; another roller-coaster is entirely underground. Meals, snacks, shop, disabled access; open wknds and school hols (not Christmas) Easter–Oct, and daily Jun–early Sept; (01765) 635321; £12.95. There's an adjacent factory shopping village, open all year.

The Staveley Arms does decent food.

20. Captain Cook, country crafts and animals

Captain Cook Birthplace Museum (Stewart Park, Marton, 3m S of Middlesbrough) Lots that will appeal to children at this interesting museum, which looks at the life and voyages of Captain Cook with hands-on displays, computer interactives and films; the landscaped grounds are impressive too. Meals, snacks, shop, disabled access; cl Mon (exc bank hols and school hols), 25–26 Dec, 1 Jan; (01642) 311211; £2.40. The nearby Apple Tree has good food.

Newham Grange Leisure Farm (Coulby Newham, off A174) Rare breeds and other animals, an agricultural museum with craft displays, reconstructed vet's surgery and saddler's shop, play and picnic areas. Snacks, shop, disabled access; usually only cl wkdys Oct–Feb; (01642) 300202; £1.80.

As an alternative to Newham Grange and to keep the seafaring mood, you could complete the day with a trip over to **Saltburn-by-the-Sea**. Originally a superior Victorian seaside resort, this still has traces of those days in the Italianate valley garden and the water-operated sloping tramway by the pier. The Ship Inn, a good pub right by the boats pulled up on the beach, is probably the most ancient building. Beside it is a smuggling heritage centre, with a vivid interactive exhibition on the town's smuggling history, housed in old seaside cottages. Shop; cl Oct–Mar; (01642) 444318; *£1.90. The beach is sheltered by the great headland of Warsett Hill to the S, and a grand section of the well signed Cleveland Way long-distance path takes walkers over this and beyond.

21. Gore and more

York Dungeon (Clifford St, York) Carefully researched exploration of 2,000 years of superstition, torture and various forms of death, full of grue and gore. There's an extensive Guy Fawkes Experience and Dick Turpin Story, also an exhibition on the Plague. Snacks, shop, some disabled access; cl 25 Dec; (01904) 632599; *£6.95.

Castle Museum (Tower St) In 18th-c prison buildings on the site of the former castle (part of the outer wall still stands), this is one of the best social history museums in the country, with a huge range of everyday objects from the past four centuries shown in convincingly reconstructed real-life settings, from Edwardian streets to prison cells and more contemporary living rooms. There's even a watermill, by the river outside. They have one of only three Anglo-Saxon helmets in the world, found here in York in the 1980s. Best out of term-time. Shop, disabled access ground floor only; cl 25–26 Dec, 1 Jan; (01904) 653611; £5.75.

Clifford's Tower (Tower St) This former castle keep is perhaps York's most interesting building after the Minster. You can walk around the top of the walls (children especially like this bit), which enclose a garden, and there are good views of the city. It gets its name from Roger Clifford, who was hanged from the tower in chains. There's an unusual Lowry painting of the tower in the City Art Gallery (see entry above). Shop; cl 24–26 Dec, 1 Jan; (01904) 646940; £2. EH.

The Tudor Masons Arms is a handy stop.

The whole centre of York, ringed by strollable 13th-c city walls, is virtually traffic-free – the biggest such area in any similarly-sized European city. It's full of lovely medieval buildings and twisting alleys, interesting shops and lots of lively cafés, pubs and bars. You can do the circuit of the 13th-c city walls and their many towers in a couple of hours or so, mostly on top. One of the best stretches, with good views of the Minster, is between the Monk Bar and Bootham Bar. If you plan on doing the whole circuit it's a good idea to rent one of the Walkman guides available at the helpful tourist office (Exhibition Sq); there's also a good fun guided ghost walk at 7.30pm (exc 24–31 Dec) beginning at the Shambles;

(01904) 608700; £3. The York Pass is worth considering if you plan to visit lots of sites in one go; £21 for a day, it applies to more than 30 of the city's attractions. Coming by train, you can exploit the First Stop York by Train scheme, which offers discounts on many of the major attractions, restaurants, and places to stay. The campaign runs Oct–Apr, with leaflets from main line railway stations or the tourist office.

22. National Railway Museum

(Leeman Rd, York) Somewhere to spend a whole day, celebrating the great railway age with lots of panache; the background sounds and smells of a steam-era station add to the atmosphere. The centrepiece is the spectacular great hall, in which tracks radiate from a central turntable with a display of two dozen great locomotives from the museum's huge collection. Children might get the most out of the Interactive Learning Centre, where plenty of hands-on exhibits and activities vividly explain how trains and railways work, though they're also bound to relish the chance to build their own model train in the excellent Works wing, where you can also watch the engineers and craftsmen as they carry out conservation work. The Working Railway looks at the technology behind Britain's rail network, with a live link to York station's signal box. A miniature railway operates most wknds and school hols, with steam train rides during school hols. You can usually get a road train from York Minster to the museum every day in summer. Meals, snacks (and picnic areas), shop, disabled access; cl 24–26 Dec; (01904) 621261; £7.50, free for children and OAPs. Their all-day car park costs £3.

23. Birds by the hundred thousand

Bempton Cliffs (Bempton) The RSPB bird reserve here has the biggest colony of seabirds in the country, with up to a quarter of a million of them nesting in the cliffs. Best views of puffins Jun–July, but plenty of skuas and shearwaters later in summer, with wknd boat trips from Flamborough (North Landing) or Bridlington, though what you'll see depends on the weather. Snacks, shop, some disabled access; visitor centre cl all Jan, wknds Dec and Feb; (01262) 851179 – book well ahead for the boats; £3 car parking charge.

    Sewerby Hall (NE edge of Bridlington) In spacious parkland right on the coast, with a miniature zoo and aviary (good for children), and a charming garden. The elegant early 18th-c house includes some Amy Johnson memorabilia – the pioneer aviator lived nearby. Snacks, shop, disabled access (but not to the hall); grounds open daily all year, house cl Weds–Fri end Oct–Mar, 24 Dec–mid-Feb; (01262) 673769; £3.10.

24. The Deep

(Tower St, Sammy's Point, Hull) This wasn't yet open at the time of writing but we really like the sound of this hi-tech new exhibition on the sea, which should offer far more than your average aquarium. Yorkshire has had a number of high-profile attractions opening in recent years, and not all have been a success, but so much effort and time have been invested in this one already (£45.5 million at the last count), that we're sticking our neck out and guessing The Deep will make quite a splash. Recent visitors to Hull can't have missed work on the astonishing building; all the walls are at an angle, and the main bit will jut out 30 metres (100 ft) above the Humber estuary. If the plans are to be believed (it wasn't finished on our last trip), the only thing you can compare it to is the sort of rocket launcher that comes out of the side of buildings or islands in old sci-fi films. Inside, the focus will be on the world's oceans: how they were formed, how marine life has developed, and how they're affected by outer space, the equator, and by man; lots of interactives are promised, and the latest lighting and effects will bring it all to life. The Polar Galley will have a pair of real ice walls, and they'll have around 500 species of fish from all over the planet, some of which will take their chances alongside the sharks in their showpiece aquarium, said to be the deepest in the world. As you'd expect, there'll be a walk-through tunnel at the bottom, the selling point being that there'll be nine metres of water above you – far more than normal, allowing greater freedom for the creatures to move around as they would at sea. A deep-sea base down here will have activities and experiments, inc the chance to pilot a submarine or work out a crew's diet (actors will take the part of the crew), and at the end a glass lift will whizz you back up to the surface, as though you were in a submarine. A new bridge will link the centre with the town. Meals, snacks, shop, disabled access; best to ring for the exact opening date, after which they'll be open every day exc 25 Dec; (01482) 381000; *£6 adults, £4 children.

25. A free day out in Hull

Streetlife Museum (High St) Reopened in early 2002 following extensive refurbishment, this substantial collection is devoted mainly to local public transport and bicycles, some weird and wonderful. Improvements will include a new motor car gallery, a major extension of the carriage gallery, a larger street-scene with several new shops, and a hands-on interactive exhibition area. Shop, disabled access; cl Sun am, 25–26 am Dec, 1 Jan, and Good Fri; (01482) 613902; free.

Hull Maritime Museum (Queen Victoria Sq) This massive yet solidly stylish three-domed Victorian building has good displays on Hull's maritime history. There's a long-established section on whales and whaling, and the huge skeletons on display were mentioned in *Moby Dick*. Shop, disabled access; cl 24–26, 31 Dec and 1 Jan; (01482) 613902; free.

Hands on History (South Church Side) Formerly the Old Grammar School (Hull's oldest secular building, dating from 1583), this now houses a rapidly expanding social history collection. Shop, disabled access; open pm wknds and also wkdys in school hols; (01482) 440144; free.

Spurn Lightship (Princes Dock, Marina) Operating from the 1920s to the 1970s – interesting to go below decks and imagine being confined to this for weeks at a time, not going anywhere, tossed about in storms or blanketed in fog. Shop, cl Sun am and Oct–Mar; (01482) 613902; free.

Ferens Art Gallery (Queen Victoria Sq) Enterprisingly run general collection, with lots of maritime paintings, Dutch Old Masters and interactive children's gallery. Snacks, shop, disabled access; cl Sun am, 24–26, 31 Dec and 1 Jan; (01482) 613902; free.

26. Eureka!

(Discovery Rd, Halifax) Remarkable hands-on museum designed exclusively for children; few places are as likely to spellbind anyone between around 3 and 12. Each of the four main galleries ostensibly explores one subject, but in fact covers a multitude of topics and ideas. Particular highlights are the broad-based Things Gallery, full of bright colours and images, the communications gallery (you can put your picture on a front page, save a yacht in distress, or read the TV news), and Living and Working Together, where children try their hand at grown-up activities like filling a car with petrol at the garage, working in a shop or bank, or making a meal in the kitchen. Easy to see why in the nine years it's been open Eureka! has won just about every award going, from Most Parent Friendly and Best Customer Care to several for Loo of the Year. Meals, snacks, shop, disabled access; cl 24–26 Dec; (01426) 983191; £5.50.

Shibden Hall & Folk Museum (Godley Lane, off A58 just E of Halifax) Excellently refurbished 15th-c house, each room illustrating a different period from its history. In the barn a folk museum has an interesting collection of horse-drawn vehicles, while outside are reconstructed 19th-c workshops, a cottage and even a pub. Boating lake, miniature railway, play area and woodland walks in the 90-acre parkland. For many this is a real Halifax highlight. Snacks, shop, limited disabled access; cl Sun am, and 25 Dec–2 Jan; (01422) 352246; £2.50.

The charming 17th-c waterside Shibden Mill (Shibden – off A647 NE) has good food.

27. Inside film and TV, horse-drawn trams, and all about colour

National Museum of Photography, Film and Television (Princes View, Bradford) Eight galleries take in everything from John Logie Baird to the toys from *Play School*. Among the three million items kept here are three key 'firsts': the world's first negative, the earliest television footage, and what's generally considered the first example of moving pictures – Louis Le Prince's 1888 film of Leeds Bridge. Wallace and Gromit and Morph explain the secrets of animation, and you can try your hand at operating a camera or reading the news. Other highlights are the intriguing photography gallery, which includes the cameras used to create the Cottingley fairies, and a stunning gallery showcases the latest digital technology, where you can experiment with virtual reality. The five storeys high IMAX screen regularly shows 3D and other films, and more conventionally sized cinemas offer films from around the world. Meals and snacks (and a room to eat packed lunches), excellent shop, disabled access; cl Mon (exc bank hols and school summer hols), 25 Dec; (01274) 202030; free. IMAX cinema is £5.80.

Industrial Museum (Moorside Rd, Eccleshill, Bradford) Former spinning mill well illustrating the growth of the worsted textile industry. Horse-drawn trams carry you up and down the Victorian street, which is complete with workers' cottages, mill owner's house and working Victorian stables with shire horses. Meals, snacks, shop, disabled access; cl Sun am, and all day Mon (exc bank hols), 25–26 Dec, 1 Jan, Good Fri; (01274) 631756; free.

Colour Museum (Grattan Rd, Bradford) Imaginative study of the use and perception of colour, with interactive displays on the effects of light and colour in general, and particularly the story of dyeing and textile printing. Shop, disabled access; cl Sun, Mon, and 23 Dec–1 Jan; (01274) 390955; £1.75.

Useful pub lunch places include the Fountain (Heaton Rd), Office (off City St) and Rams Revenge (Kirkgate).

28. Arms, armour and the world's oldest railway

Royal Armouries Museum (Clarence Dock, Waterfront, Leeds) A far cry from the average military museum, this houses the National Museum of Arms and Armour, previously displayed at the Tower of London, but shown off here in a radically different way. It's almost completely interactive, with hi-tech effects and push-button displays, and plenty of costumed demonstrations showing not just how weapons were made and used, but how they affected everyday life; children can try on costumes and helmets, or even test their aim with a crossbow. The building's design is stunning (don't miss the breathtaking Hall of Steel, with 3,000 pieces of gleaming arms and armour on the walls), but the most spectacular feature is outside: the country's only full-size authentically re-created tiltyard, with dramatic exhibitions of jousting, fencing, duelling, and hunting dogs and birds of prey. An inside display area often has martial arts displays, and there are demonstrations of traditional skills in the Craft Court. Meals and snacks, shop, good disabled access; cl 24–25 Dec; (0113) 2201999; £4.90 on the door, but you can get tickets for £3.50 from the Tourist Information Centre.

Middleton Railway Running from Turnstall Rd to Middleton Park, this is the oldest running railway in the world and was the first to be authorised by Parliament in 1758. With a picnic area, fishing, nature trail and playgrounds as well as the trains, there's plenty for families here. Snacks, shop, disabled access; diesel or steam trains most wknds and bank hols Apr–Christmas; (0113) 271 0320 or www.middletonrailway.org.uk for timetable; £2.50.

29. Old medicine, a romantic ruin, and a tropical world

Thackray Medical Museum (Beckett St, Leeds) This dynamic museum is at St James's Hospital (featured in the TV series *Jimmy's*). The emphasis is more social history than science, but there are interactive displays on how the body works, and good reconstructions showing the progress of medical care in Britain, inc some deliciously gruesome parts on surgery before the development of anaesthetics; children particularly like the part where they pick a character, then discover their fate as they work their way around the museum. Snacks, shop, disabled access; cl Mon (exc bank and school hols), 24–26, 31 Dec, 1 Jan; (0113) 244 4343; £4.40, £14 family ticket.

Abbey House (off A65, 2m NW of Leeds centre) You can wander freely through the re-created Victorian streets at this enjoyable museum, and right through some of the shops. There's an interactive gallery on childhood (some good games and interesting facts here), and another gallery shows what life would have been like as a medieval monk. Outside are gardens, a play area, and picnic tables. Shop, snacks, disabled access; cl all Mon, am wknds, 25–26 Dec, and 1 Jan; (0113) 230 5492; £3. Opposite are the ruins of 12th-c **Kirkstall Abbey**, one of Britain's best-preserved Cistercian monasteries; cl 25–26 Dec, 1 Jan, and Easter; (0113) 230 5492; free.

Roundhay Park (off A58) 700 acres of rolling parkland, well known for concerts and events. On Princes Avenue here the Canal Gardens are a very pleasant and peaceful corner of the city, with several national flower collections (inc dahlias and violas), lots of roses, and ornamental wildfowl; free. Its gem is **Tropical World**, a huge conservatory with the biggest collection of tropical plants outside Kew, along with all sorts of exotic trees, reptiles, fish, birds and butterflies, in careful re-creations of their natural settings. Meals, snacks, shop, disabled access; cl 25 Dec; (0113) 266 1850; £2.

The nearby Roundhay dining pub has very cheap food.

30. From Victorian melodrama to hands-on science

Elsecar Heritage Centre (Wath Rd, Elsecar) Developing centre in restored industrial workshops. Lots to see inc a hands-on science centre, a history centre where you can dress up and star in a Victorian melodrama, a beam engine and craft workshops. On summer Suns a steam train runs to the Hemingfield Basin. Meals, snacks, shop, disabled access; cl 25 Dec–2 Jan; (01226) 740203; £3.25 science centre, £1 history centre, £2.50 train, or £5.25 for all.

The Old Moor Inn over at Broom Hill (B6273 N of Brampton) has good value home cooking.

31. Environmental action below a great fortress

Earth Centre (Denaby Main) Perhaps the most ambitious of all the country's environmental centres, this Millennium Commission project has witnessed the redevelopment over the last decade or so of more than 400 acres left derelict by the decline of the coal industry. Rarely busy, the centre aims to promote environmental issues in an enjoyable way through a range of attractions taking in an interactive nature trail (with pond-dipping, eco-friendly games and an area designed to stimulate all your senses along the way), galleries looking at the history and future of the planet's development, and specially themed gardens dotted with often bizarre-looking constructions; also a fun adventure playground inc a 16-metre (52-ft) play tower. Meals, snacks, shop, disabled access; cl 24–26 Dec; (01709) 512000; £3.95.

Overlooking it is 12th-c **Conisbrough Castle**, mightily impressive with its uniquely designed 27-metre (90 ft) keep – circular, with six buttresses and a curtain wall with solid round towers. An added roof and floors re-create something of the original feel, and there's a good audio-visual show; special events in summer. Snacks, craft shop, limited disabled access; cl 24–26 Dec, 1 Jan; (01709) 863329; £3; EH. Sir Walter Scott set much of *Ivanhoe* here, writing the novel while staying at the Boat at Sprotbrough nearby; then a riverside farm, it's now a popular dining pub.

32. Magna

(off A6178, SW of Rotherham centre; Templeborough) Beautifully designed in an awesome former steel works, this new centre puts a colourful spin on the story of the steel industry. It has four themed pavilions based around the main elements used in steel-making: Earth, housed in the basement, re-creates the drama of working in a quarry, Air is an inflated structure, designed to look like an airship hovering over the main factory floor, Water gives children plenty of excuses to soak their parents, and Fire, set around a giant live flame, uses audio-visual displays to illustrate how man has controlled fire for his benefit, as well as its explosive (and destructive) possibilities. Plenty of emphasis on hands-on activities and interactive experiences. Meals, snacks, shop, disabled access; cl 24–25 Dec; (01709) 720002; £6.99.

33. Hand-feed the animals and watch the craftsmen

Elsham Hall Country & Wildlife Park (Elsham) As well as the sheep, goats and donkeys you might expect, there are llamas, snakes and spiders, some of which you can stroke or feed. Especially unusual is the carp-feeding jetty, where monster-sized fish will feed straight from your hand. They have a talk and demonstration of some of their mini-beasts every day at 1 o'clock, then at 2, weather permitting, they show off some of their birds of prey. Most things are outside, so it's best to visit on a dry day. There's a craft centre, with demonstrations by a potter, wood-turner and blacksmith, an arboretum, barn theatre, woodland garden, and plenty of space to let off steam. An adventure playground has sections for different age groups. Special events include lambing days in spring. Meals and snacks (they do a good Sunday lunch), picnic area, shops, garden centre, disabled access; cl Mon and Tues (exc bank and school hols), and all mid-Sept–Easter; (01652) 688698; £4.50.

34. Life on the trawlers

National Fishing Heritage Centre (Alexandra Dock, Grimsby)

Displays recalling the experiences of a trawlerman of the mid-1950s take you from the back streets of Grimsby, to the fishing grounds of the Arctic Circle and back. Everything in the main centre is under cover, but outside there are enjoyable guided tours of a real trawler, the *Ross Tiger*, led by a former trawlerman. Meals, snacks, shop, disabled access (not to *Ross Tiger*); cl Fri and Oct–Mar; (01472) 323345; £4.95.

To fill out a day, this could be coupled with any of the places we recommend in adjoining Cleethorpes, under Pleasure Island (next page). Also in Cleethorpes is the **Humber Estuary Discovery Centre** (Kings Rd), an unusual spiral-shaped building inspired by seashells. This gives an interactive journey through time (Cleethorpes lies on the Prime Meridian which divides East from West), looking at local natural and social history; also aquarium and telescopes for bird- and ship-spotting on the Humber estuary. Snacks, shop, disabled access; cl 25–26 Dec, 1 Jan; (01472) 323232; £1.95.

35. Pleasure Island

(Kings Rd, Cleethorpes) Enough to keep a family entertained for the day, this theme park has lots of suitably scary rides (inc a terrifying new one called Hyper Blaster, which involves being shot up and down a 90-ft tower), also children's rides, cabaret and various animal shows. Meals, snacks, shop, disabled access; cl end Oct–Apr; (01472) 211511; £10.

This big traditional seaside resort has extensive gently shelving tidal sands, and some of the seafront buildings are being restored to their Victorian/Edwardian elegance. A light railway runs from Lakeside Station (Kings Rd) for a gentle mile through the local scenery. Snacks, shop, disabled coach; cl wkdys Oct–Easter (01472) 604657; £2. Also at Lakeside, Jungle has tropical wildlife from anacondas and iguanas to monkeys and parakeets. There are new llamas and an alligator, plus a children's farm and guinea-pig village; snacks, shop, disabled access; cl 25 Dec; (01472) 291998; £3.

36. Fantasy Island

(Sea Lane, Ingoldmells) More elaborate than your average fairground, and largely unaffected by the weather, this dynamic place also impresses with its parent-friendly pricing system, and its unusual design. Most of the rides and other features are inside, with thatched buildings and palm trees nestling under a giant pyramid, though as the site rapidly expands a number of rides are springing up outside too. It doesn't cost anything to wander round: you pay for rides (with tokens) only as you go on them, so it's easy to keep coming in and out over time rather than rushing round trying to do everything at once; the beach is just opposite. The most exciting ride is the Millennium roller-coaster, which goes through 360-degree loops around the outside of the pyramid, at heights of 46 metres (150 ft) and a speed of around 100 mph. They add things every year; a huge £28 million suspended roller-coaster Odyssey is set to open in 2002, with the longest drop in Europe. Other highlights include a cross between a roller-coaster and a waltzer, an IMAX simulator creating the illusion of rides through a fun house, a haunted castle, and even through space (the screen is all around you, and your seat slides towards it as well as shaking about all over the place), the balloon flight, with authentically created computer-controlled balloons soaring around the pyramid, a sail-through aquarium, exploding volcano and two water rides – one quite long, the other rather wet. Plenty for younger children, inc a train ride through the world of the Jellikins, and live shows with TV characters from Pinky and Perky to the Butt Ugly Martians. Outside are a big play area for the under-5s, and a huge market, with around 780 stalls. Lots of places to eat (mostly fast food from high street names, though of course you can nip out for lunch and come back later), disabled access; open wknds and school hols Mar–Apr, then daily till the end of Oct; (01754) 872030; free admission to park, then rides charged separately – ride tokens are 60p each, with the most elaborate rides usually costing three or four tokens; the Millennium roller-coaster uses a special token which costs £3. It's open very late in the main season – till 11pm Fri/Sat.

37. Seals, seabirds and more

Natureland Seal Sanctuary (North Parade, Skegness) Opposite the beach, this rewarding place is renowned for its seal-rescuing activities. It's fascinating to watch the seals performing tricks – they aren't trained in any way, they just like showing off. Feeding times are announced over the public address system, and other animals include penguins, crocodiles, snakes, insects, tropical birds and free-flying butterflies May–Sept; also pets corner, tropical aquarium and farmyard animals. You can see almost everything from covered walkways if it rains. Snacks, shop, disabled access; cl 25–26 Dec, 1 Jan; (01754) 764345; £4.25.

Church Farm Museum (Church Rd S) Cluster of restored farmyard buildings and cottage provides a good re-creation of daily farm life at the end of the 19th c, also craft demonstrations and special events. Snacks, shop, limited disabled access; cl Nov–Mar; (01754) 766658; £1.

Gibraltar Point Nature Reserve (Gibraltar Rd) 1,000 acres of sandy and muddy seashore stretching 3m S from Skegness to the mouth of the Wash. The impressive complex of sand dunes and saltmarsh is good for bird-watching, and home to a wide variety of wildlife; guided walks and events in summer. Summer snacks, shop, disabled access to visitor centre and some hides; reserve open all year, visitor centre cl wkdys Nov–May; (01754) 762677; free (parking £2 in high season).

The comfortable old Vine Hotel on the southern edge of Skegness was here long before the resort, welcoming Tennyson among others; it's pleasant for lunch. There's a good bathing beach (and outdoor swimming pool).

38. Fun for the youngest ones

Sundown Adventureland (Treswell Rd, Rampton; N of A57) Popular with readers, this cheerful little leisure park is best for children between around 4 and 8. It's full of decent life-size representations and tableaux of stories and fairy-tales, from the Wild West to the Three Little Pigs. There are gentle rides and several themed play areas, one under cover (height restrictions apply in here). Good Christmas displays, when every child gets a present from Santa. Snacks (mostly fast food), shop, some disabled access; cl 25–26 Dec, wkdys Jan–mid-Feb; (01777) 248274; £5.25 everyone over 2.

The Moth & Lantern at nearby Cottam has good value family food, and a pets corner.

39. Sherwood Forest and Robin Hood

Sherwood Forest Farm Park (Lamb Pens Farm, off A6075, Edwinstowe) Unusual breeds of traditional farm animals, water buffalo and wallabies, pets corner, and colourful waterfowl on a sizeable lake. Also an owl garden, adventure playground (with a separate section for the under-5s), and picnic area. They usually have some activities in a barn, but it's very much a place for fine weather. Special events may include an Easter treasure hunt, and demonstrations of sheep shearing and spinning (best to check exact dates); home-baked teas and snacks, shop, mostly disabled access (can be tricky around the lakes); open daily Easter–mid-Oct; (01623) 823558; £4, children £2.75.

Sherwood Forest Visitor Centre (Edwinstowe) With an exhibition on Robin Hood, the visitor centre is a good springboard for the forest itself, only a fraction of what it once was (it used to cover a fifth of the county) but still miles across, though the heathland that Robin himself would have known has largely been swallowed up either by farmland or by forestry plantation. Good waymarked paths and footpaths, the most popular being to the Major Oak (a huge tree in the heart of the forest). Meals, snacks, shop, disabled access; park entry free, car park £1.50. The Sherwood Forest Art and Craft Centre nearby has 16 craft studios housed in a purpose-built centre; cl Mon and Tues Oct–Mar.

Nr the village church (supposedly where Robin Hood and Maid Marian were married), the Black Swan is handy for something to eat.

40. How farming works today

White Post Modern Farm Centre (A614, 1m W of Farnsfield) This bustling modern working farm has everything from a mouse town to llamas, quails, snakes and fish. Especially good fun is their goat mountain, which lets goats combine two of their favourite activities, climbing and eating. There's also an enjoyable show, where you're talked through a farmer's year with the help of pigs, rabbits, ducks and rats. You can buy food for many of the animals, and younger visitors can hold chicks and ducklings, or fuss the guinea-pigs and rabbits in the farmyard. They're particularly strong on pigs, and you can always watch eggs hatching in their huge incubator. Most displays and animals move indoors if the weather is bad, and there's an indoor sand pit. Lots of activities in the field, and along with farm trails and pony rides there's also a bat house, aviary, and reptile handling sessions. They sell various insects and reptiles, and have a Reptile Hotel to look after them while you're on holiday. Dogs can't come into the farm, but can be left in attended kennels. Meals, snacks, heated picnic area, good farm shop, disabled access; (01623) 882977; £4.95.

The Red Lion in the village, with a play area in its garden, is popular for lunch.

41. Cops and robbers – try your hand at both

Galleries of Justice (Shire Hall, High Pavement, Nottingham) The grim realities of a 19th-c trial and prison life are re-enacted with real verve at this first-rate centre, set around two Victorian courtrooms in use right through to 1986. In recent years the place has expanded to include fascinating displays on justice through the ages, but the centrepiece remains the excellent trial, designed very much to entertain children. On arrival they're given a criminal identity number and sent for trial in the Criminal Court. It's hardly giving the game away to say that the verdict is always guilty, but what will be the sentence? Public flogging, transportation to a penal colony – or even execution? 'Prisoners' are led down to the cells, where costumed interpreters posing as warders, gaolers and a fellow prisoner prepare them for their fate. Being locked in a cell or working a treadmill is a real eye-opener for older children (it's not ideal for younger ones); they won't come out hardened felons. The other highlight is an equally arresting police station experience, where you can try your hand at cracking a murder case. More traditional displays examine the role of prisons and other legal issues; they have the world's largest collection of handcuffs and other restraints. Also interesting temporary exhibitions, which in the last year have covered everything from Lord Lucan to Judge Dredd. As enjoyable as they're informative, the galleries are all under cover, so they're a good bet all year round; a visit can easily stretch out to a half day. Meals, snacks, shop, some disabled access; cl Mon (exc bank hols), and 24–26 Dec, 1 Jan; (0115) 952 0555; £6.95 adults, £5.25 children 4–14. The family ticket (two adults, two children) is good value at £19.95.

Caves of Nottingham (Drury Walk) Tour with taped commentary of 750-yr-old caverns beneath a busy modern shopping centre, through an underground tannery, Victorian slum, air raid shelters, and pub cellars. Shop; cl 24–26 Dec, 1 Jan and Easter Sun; (0115) 924 1424; £3.75.

Fellows Morton & Clayton (Canal St), with waterside tables, has good value food; on a rainy day the Olde Trip to Jerusalem (Brewhouse Yard), with its ancient rooms built into the rock caverns below the Castle, might be more fun for a family lunch.

42. Britain's biggest cave

Peak Cavern (Castleton) Right in the village, this is the biggest natural cavern in the country and really does seem huge – the entrance hall is so large it used to house an entire village; there are no significant stalagtites or stalagmites. From there it's a half-mile walk along subterranean passageways to the Great Cave, 45 by 27 metres (150 ft wide, 90 ft long). By the time you reach the Devil's Staircase you'll be nearly 140 metres (450 ft) underground. Rope-making demonstrations; snacks, shop; cl wkdys Nov–Easter; (01433) 620285; £5.

Peveril Castle (Castleton) This ruined fortress dominates the village. Built high above in the 11th c, it gives magnificent views. Shop, snacks; cl Mon and Tues in Nov–Mar, 24–26 Dec and 1 Jan; (01433) 620613; £2.30; EH.

In Castleton there's decent food at the Rose Cottage, Castle, George and Olde Nags Head (the craft shop opp here has interesting things made from blue john, the unique semi-precious stone found only around here), and in the pretty nearby village of Hope the Cheshire Cheese is good.

The most varied walks in the High Peak are found around Castleton and Hope. The great walk here takes in Castleton, the Lose Hill/Mam Tor ridge, the caves, and Winnats Pass; Mam Tor is so shaly and prone to landslips that it's dubbed the Shivering Mountain – the abandoned section of the A625 is a testament to the victory of the mountain over man. Cave Dale is an optional side trip from the back of Castleton. Quarrying has had an unfortunate effect on the local landscape, and limits walks further afield, though there are some pleasant walks to be had in the gentler high pastures of the limestone country to the south.

An alternative for hiking-minded families is to go to Edale, which is famous as the start of the 256-mile Pennine Way to the Scottish border. It has a good information centre, and decent food in the Old Nags Head. It tends to be packed with expectant long-distance walkers on Sunday mornings. This can be the start for half-day walks that quite quickly take you up through the stone-walled pastures of the valley on to the edge of the dark plateau of the Dark Peak above. The track signed as the alternative Pennine Way route up Jacob's Ladder is easier to find, and has more to see (inc some strange weathered rocks and an ancient cross), than the official Pennine Way plod across a huge blanket bog.

43. Chatsworth

(off B6012) Perhaps surprisingly, this splendid estate on the banks of the River Derwent has almost as much appeal for children as it has for adults, with enough to keep most ages happy for longer than you'd think. The first-class adventure playground is perhaps the highlight for younger visitors: big, well constructed and prettily set, it has an elaborate spiral chute, swings, and sand and water play areas, with commando wires and ropewalks for older children. It's very well supervised, with plenty of seats for adults. A working farmyard has plenty of opportunities to get close to cows, sheep, pigs and horses, as well as useful demonstrations of how they work the extensive estate; milking demonstrations every afternoon at 3.30, and you can join in feeding the trout. There's also a maze, and they're delightfully unstuffy about letting children play in the long cascade that runs down to the house; on a hot day, it's perfect for toddlers to paddle in. The house itself — for adults one of the country's most deeply satisfying, with more to see than at many of its peers — has been home to the Duke of Devonshire's family for nearly 450 years. Sumptuously furnished, the 26 rooms on display show off a superb collection of fine arts, with memorable paintings by Rembrandt and Van Dyck, and all sorts of intriguing decorative details. There are usually fewer people around as the afternoon wears on. A set of nine Regency bedrooms is also usually open for a small extra charge. Private guided tours are available by prior arrangement (extra charge). The lovely gardens cover 100 acres and are full of surprises; brass bands play on summer Sunday afternoons. The surrounding park was landscaped by Capability Brown, and covers 1,000 acres; well marked walks and trails. Dogs on leads are allowed. Good meals and snacks, shop, garden centre, disabled access to garden only; usually cl Nov–mid-Mar; (01246) 582204. By far the best value for families is the Family Pass, which gets two adults and up to four children into the house and garden, farmyard and adventure playground for £27. Otherwise individual charges are £7 house and garden (children £3), £4 garden only (£1.75 children), and a further £3.50 (adults and children) for the farm and adventure playground. Entry to the park is free. Car parking is £1. Also in the grounds, at Stud Farm, 1½ miles towards Pilsley, is one of England's best farm shops (they also have a branch in London). Around Chatsworth, Edensor is a very attractive estate village, and walkers have free access to the park W of the River Derwent; there is a delightful riverside walk at Calton Lees car park, N to Chatsworth bridge and Edensor. The B6012 (busy in summer) has pleasant views, and the Devonshire Arms at Beeley has good food all day.

44. Underground spectacular

Heights of Abraham Country Park (Matlock Bath) Derbyshire is full of stunning show caverns, but few are as good for families, and none can boast as thrilling an introduction as the one here: cable cars whisk you up from the Derwent Valley to a 60-acre country park, with dramatic views over the ancient limestone gorge (not to mention a railway and the busy A6). At the end of the 5-minute trip a multi-media show explains how the rock was formed 325 million years ago, then guides escort you into the two show caverns. Outside are nature trails, the Prospect Tower to climb and a few play areas (inc a maze), as well as great views and nicely laid out woodland walks; usually clown shows or similar entertainments in summer. Good meals and snacks, shop, limited disabled access – best to phone beforehand; open most wknds mid-Feb–Easter (best to check first as dates can depend on the weather), then daily mid-Mar–Oct; (01629) 582365; £6.80.

Matlock Bath is a pleasantly busy place, with lots to do. A

spectacular wooded cliff looks across the lower roadside town to pastures by the Derwent; up the side of the gorge, quiet lanes climb steeply past 18th- and 19th-c villas. The Temple Hotel (Temple Walk) has great views and decent food.

45. A bargain day out around Derby

Industrial Museum (Full St, Derby) Warmly praised by some readers, this restored early 18th-c silk mill and adjacent flour mill has probably the world's finest collection of Rolls-Royce aero engines, and a Power Gallery with lots of hands-on displays. Shop, disabled access; cl am Sun and bank hols, and some time over Christmas – phone to check; (01332) 255308; free. The nearby Old Silk Mill is an interesting pub, open all day.

    Pickfords House Museum (Friargate) Gives a very good idea of 18th-c domestic life, with period furnished rooms and Georgian garden; also costume display and a collection of toy theatres. Shop, some disabled access and video with subtitles; cl Sun and bank hol am, and over Christmas – phone to check; (01332) 255363; free.

    Elvaston Castle Country Park (B5010, Elvaston) 200 acres of lovely 19th-c landscaped parkland, with formal and Old English gardens, wooded walks, and wildfowl on the ornamental lake. Also museum with traditional craft workshops, and nature trails. Meals, snacks, shop, disabled access; open all year, but museum open only Weds–Sat pms plus Sun and bank hols May–Oct (01332) 571342; museum £1.20, car park 70p wkdys, £1.30 wknds. Nearby Shardlow, an interesting canal-based village, has useful lunch places if you don't feel like a picnic.

46. Rides and rambles: a day out around Ilkeston

American Adventure Theme Park (Pit Lane, Ilkeston) Excellent theme park with around 100 rides and attractions; all supposedly have an American theme, though this can be rather tenuous – ever so English Sooty stars in a Wild West show. Highlights include the SkyCoaster, at 61 metres (200 ft) the UK's biggest freefall ride, a 13-metre (42 ft) drop at 62 mph on the Nightmare Niagara triple log flume, and the Missile, a stomach-churning roller-coaster that twists and turns at unfeasible angles, before going the whole route again backwards. Live shows include a Wild West saloon and a Mexican fiesta, and there's a huge indoor play area for younger children; some extra charges for go-karts, crazy golf and so on. Meals, snacks, shops, good disabled access; cl Nov–early Apr; (01773) 531521; £13.50 (children under 1 metre, free).

   Shipley Country Park Medieval estate developed and landscaped in the 18th c, with 600 acres of woodland, lakes and fields. A pleasant place to wander or for picnics, with railway lines transformed into leafy walkways. Snacks, shop, disabled access; visitor centre cl 25 Dec; (01773) 719961; free.

47. Playing potter, and a very approachable zoo

Gladstone Pottery Museum (Uttoxeter Rd, Longton, Stoke-on-Trent) Particularly engrossing, a complete Victorian pottery made much more appealing to families over the last few years, with lively demonstrations and interpretation, and a new display of historic loos. The museum's very much hands-on, and even hands-in – they're quite keen to get your fingers round the clay, and children love throwing pots (though it can work out expensive as all 'makes' have to be bought). It's quite possible to spend up to half a day here. Meals, snacks, shop, mostly disabled access; cl Christmas week; (01782) 319232; £3.95.

Blackbrook Zoological Park (Winkhill) Unusual species and aviaries, as well as waterfowl, insects and reptiles, under-5s' playroom and children's farm – all much enjoyed by readers. Tearooms, shop, good disabled access; cl 25–26, 31 Dec, 1 Jan; (01538) 308293; £5.50. At pretty Waterhouses nearby you can hire bikes from the Old Station Car Park; (01538) 308609; around £7 for three hrs.

The attractively set Cross there has decent food. An alternative for a family lunch is the riverside Jervis Arms at Onecote, with pygmy goats and a play area.

48. Alton Towers

(Alton, off B5032) Britain's best theme park, where very young children are looked after just as well as daredevil teenagers, and they're always adding something new: watch out in 2002 for a new £15 million roller-coaster, where you'll be flung round as you lie in a position not unlike Superman in full flight. Nice. Of course there are downsides: a visit here needs a fair amount of planning to get the best value, and you'll need to arrive first thing just to stand a chance of getting round everything. Many features do still have queues; the average wait is 10 mins, but can be much longer. They've tried to cut the wait for the most popular rides, fearsome roller-coasters Nemesis and Oblivion. Book in advance and you're let into the park early, so you can go on these two before the crowds arrive. And at other times you can get a timed ticket, which should limit the wait to 20 mins. Not sure what you're letting yourself in for? Oblivion is a three-minute horror climaxing in a 70mph vertical drop, and Nemesis whisks you through unfeasible angles at a greater G-force than experienced by astronauts in a rocket launch; both are unsuitable for anyone under 1.4 metres (4½ ft). Other highlights (if you like that sort of thing) are a ride that spins you through three complete loops before dangling several storeys above ground (while being attacked by jets of water from handily placed fountains), and the spooky new Hex, a hi-tech haunted house. Several areas are aimed specifically at younger children; Storybook Land has gentler rides suited to under-7s (toddlers love the singing barn), and live shows feature Barney, the inexplicably popular purple dinosaur (pre-booked tickets guarantee you front-row seats). Dozens of other attractions, from log flumes to lovely extensive gardens that anywhere else would probably be worth a look in their own right. Staying at their splendidly zany hotel also gets you into the park half an hour or so before the main gates open; there's a bizarre cross between a galleon and a hot-air balloon in the lobby. It's by no means a cheap day out, but the presentation and facilities are excellent: if you don't normally like theme parks, you may be pleasantly surprised. They usually end the season with a series of spectacular firework displays. Meals, snacks, shop, disabled access (on most rides too); open mid-Mar–early Nov; (01538) 702200; normal full price entry is £23 for adults, and £19 children aged 4–12, with a family ticket – two adults and two children, or one adult and three children – knocking a bit off that at £70. Booking in advance, either by phone or online at www.alton-towers.com, will usually save a few more pounds. They've introduced off-peak tickets that are £5 cheaper than normal; these are available wkdys out of season, so not great for children, but ideal for adults free to flee the office. If you don't see it all in a day and want to come back, you can usually buy a good value second day's entry from any of the information points around the park.

49. Shugborough Hall

(A513, Shugborough) Imposing ancestral home of the Earls of Lichfield, begun in the late 17th c, enlarged in the 18th, and now housing the County Museum; magnificent state rooms, restored working kitchens, interesting puppet collection, and exhibition of the present Earl's photography. The park has a variety of unusual neo-classical monuments, working rare-breeds farm, and restored corn mill. Meals, snacks, shop, disabled access; open Easter–Sept, plus Sun in Oct; (01889) 881388; entry to estate £2, museum and servants' quarters £4.50, house £4.50, farm £2.50; NT. An all-in ticket is quite expensive at £9 – better value on one of their special event days, when there are more activities (such as hands-on Victorian cookery displays) for no extra cost.

There are interesting canal walks from nearby Great Haywood, where you can find the longest packhorse bridge in the country. The canalside Wolseley Arms towards Rugeley is a handy food stop. If you're coming from the M6, the Moat House at Acton Trussell is also a good place for a family lunch.

50. Rides galore, and a handsome castle

Drayton Manor Family Theme Park (off A4091 S of Tamworth) Popular theme park, with 100 rides and attractions inc a small zoo (cl 24 Dec–2 Jan; £5). Meals, snacks, shop, disabled access; cl Nov–Mar; (01827) 287979; £15. **Tamworth Castle** (off Market St) Glorious mixture of architectural styles, from the original Norman motte and bailey walls through the Elizabethan timbered hall to the fine Jacobean state apartments. Perhaps more museum than historic home, but plenty to see, with a fair amount to please children, inc high-tech talking heads. Shop, disabled access to ground floor; open Mon–Fri and pm wknds mid-Feb–Oct; (01827) 709626, £4.30.

51. 18th-century lively lads

Quarry Bank Mill & Styal Estate (Styal) Really popular with readers, this is one of the best and most extensive places in the country to get to grips with the Industrial Revolution; as you can easily spend most of a day here, it's also good value for money. The 18th-c cotton mill that's the centrepiece still produces cloth (you can buy it in the shop), and as well as demonstrations of spinning and weaving has lively exhibitions looking at factory conditions for the millworkers and their bosses. A hands-on exhibition explains how the 1840 beam engine in the original engine house was restored, while the 50-ton working water wheel remains an impressive sight. The surrounding village has carefully preserved workers' cottages, chapels and shop, and they grow rare types of fruit and vegetables in the garden. At the Apprentice House enthusiastic guides in period dress explain the lifestyle and 12-hr working days faced by young pauper children (you can even try out their beds); there are timed tickets in operation here, so it makes sense to see this bit at the start of your visit. Good woodland and riverside walks in the park and plenty of space for picnics by the river, lots of events throughout the year. Meals, snacks, shop, disabled access; cl winter Mons, apprentice house cl am wkdys, Mon during school terms; (01625) 527468; all-in ticket £6, mill only £4.80, apprentice house only £3.80; NT. The nearby Ship is pleasant for lunch.

52. Telescopes, trees and a Georgian mansion

Jodrell Bank Centre & Arboretum (off A535, nr M6 junction 18) Plenty to do at this lively place which, unusually for a working research establishment, welcomes visitors. The centrepiece is still the huge radio telescope, the second largest in the world and as big as the dome of St Paul's, but they also have a fun science centre with eight galleries examining subjects as diverse as plants, prisms and planets with hands-on displays and exhibitions; regular shows in the Planetarium (over-5s only). The 2,500 species of tree in the 35-acre arboretum are quite a contrast to the indoor exhibits and there's also an Environmental Discovery Centre and nature trails. Busy programme of events and special activities. Meals and snacks (the café has fine views of the telescope), picnic area, shop, good disabled access (outside too); (01477) 571339; cl Mon Nov–mid-Mar, and 17–21, 24–26 and 31 Dec, 1, 7–11 Jan; £4.90.

Tatton Park A few miles away just N of Knutsford is this busy estate with a handsome neo-classical Georgian mansion at its centre. (On the way the Dog at Peover Heath is a nice place to stop for a family lunch.) Magnificent collection of furnishings, porcelain and paintings (inc two Canalettos) in the opulent State rooms, and restored kitchens and servants' quarters; the Tudor Old Hall hints at the long history of the estate. The lovely grounds boast an Edwardian rose garden, Italian and Japanese gardens, orangery and fern house, leading to a big country park with mature trees, lakes, signposted walks and deer and waterfowl; you can fish or take a carriage ride. There's also a Home Farm that works as it did 60 years ago, with vintage machinery and rare breeds of animals; children's playground. You could easily spend most of an undemanding day here (good family activities in summer school hols), or take a carload for a picnic in the park. Meals, snacks, shop, some disabled access; park and gardens open all year (exc winter Mons), rest cl Mon (exc bank hols), all Nov–Mar (exc farm open Sun), mansion and Tudor Hall also cl am (mansion open some wknds in Dec with seasonal decorations); (01625) 534400; entry to park £3.50 per car (free for cyclists and pedestrians), then £3 for the mansion or gardens, farm or Tudor Hall. A ticket allowing entry for any two attractions is £4.60; NT (though as the site is

managed by the county council members still have to pay for all exc
the mansion and garden).

53. Chester's medieval heart

A great place for a visit, Chester was the site of an important fort in
Roman times, and later plentiful river traffic kept it rich. The old
centre is ringed by a medieval **town wall** that's more complete
than any other in Britain. You can walk the whole way round,
enjoying marvellous views; there are summer exhibitions in some of
the towers along the way. Within the walls, the centre, largely free
of traffic, is fun to stroll through, and children love the balconied
upper galleries in the two-storey timbered rows of medieval shops;
up here the Boot (Eastgate Row North) is an antiquated pub that
welcomes families. The tree-shaded Groves look out to the
medieval bridge over the River Dee – very photogenic and a
pleasant place for a stroll or picnic. Several companies offer boat
trips on the river from here; (01244) 325394; from £4. The Old
Harkers Arms (Russell St, down steps off City Rd) has good food
and is right on the canal; you might enjoy browsing Mike Melody
Antiques, upstairs in the same former warehouse complex.

Dewa Roman Experience (Pierpoint Lane, off Bridge St) Re-
creation of Chester's Roman heyday, with the sights, sounds and
smells of streets, fortresses, and even bathhouses. It starts off as
though you're on board a Roman galley, and at the end is an
exhibition of Roman, Saxon and medieval relics found on the site.
Shop, disabled access; cl for a few days over Christmas; (01244)
343407; £3.95.

Grosvenor Museum (Grosvenor St) You can find out lots
about Chester and its surroundings at this interesting museum, one
highlight of which is a surprisingly entertaining gallery of huge
Roman tombstones. A conservatory shop leads to a Georgian

house with restored Georgian and Victorian rooms, an art gallery, and displays of locally made silver and furniture; interactive computers and good changing exhibitions. They've recently improved their disabled access – touch-screen computers give wheelchair visitors a virtual view of the exhibits upstairs, and there are large print and Braille labels. Cl Sun am and a few days over Christmas; (01244) 402008; free.

54. Chester Zoo

(A41, 2m N of city) The biggest and undoubtedly one of the best zoos in Britain, constantly developing and improving. Its several thousand animals are housed in spacious near-natural enclosures spread over 80 acres of glorious gardens, with 11 miles of pathways. More than 200 of the species here are classed as rare or endangered, and they put a great deal of effort into breeding, so there's usually quite a range of baby animals. Highlights include the splendidly laid out Chimpanzee Island, the komodo dragons and amazon parrots in the Islands in Danger tropical habitat, the jaguar enclosure and the remarkable free-flying bat cave. There's a full programme of feeding sessions throughout the day; times can change, so best to check the day's events on the main information boards. Smaller children can pet the animals at the well organised farm. In summer a waterbus can ferry you between the attractions, and an overhead train zips around the grounds (both £1.70 extra). Meals, snacks, shops, good disabled access, tactile maps and Braille guides; cl 25 Dec; (01244) 380280; *£10.50.

55. Blue Planet Aquarium

(Ellesmere Port; off A5117 nr M53 junction 10) One of Britain's most stunning aquariums, this splendid place is run by the same people as Deep Sea World in North Queensferry, but it's even bigger and more elaborate. The creatures you'll see here are amazing, and though it does get busy, it's all very efficiently organised; an added bonus for children is that face painting is free. The most obviously dramatic feature is the 71-metre (233-ft) walk-through tunnel, surrounded by sharks, stingray, and three and a half million gallons of water; a moving walkway lets you trundle along gawping without having to look where you're going. Knowledge-able staff (many of them marine biologists) are on hand to answer questions, and give talks at various times throughout the day. Also standing out are the shows in the Aquatheatre, rather like a cinema with the screen replaced by a window into one of their biggest tanks; divers go down to feed the creatures, and use underwater microphones to chat with the audience as they do it. Try to get here a little before the shows are due to start to bag a good seat. The main displays re-create water environments from around the world, from appropriately populated trout streams and mangroves to a stretch of the Amazon; along the way touchpools give children the chance to handle star-fish and the like. As well as fish they have plenty of reptiles and insects, with some hands-on opportunities; their encounter sessions can introduce you to everything from toads and hissing cockroaches to toxic frogs. Also a couple of caymans (cousin to the crocodile), and several film and slide shows. Most displays are at a height younger children can appreciate. As at any aquarium, there can be slight congestion around some of the displays, but there's enough space here to stop that being a problem. Several nights a year they organise sleepovers for children, with fun activities and the chance to see sharks by torchlight (you'll have to prebook). Meals, snacks, shop, good disabled access; cl 25 Dec; (0151) 357 8800; £7.25 adults, £4.95 children over 3. They do various family tickets, and you can save 10% off all tickets by booking online at www.blueplanetaquarium.com. Advance booking should mean you can go straight in without needing to queue. The huge factory shopping village Cheshire Oaks next door is also a draw, with plenty of places to eat in.

56. Racing sheep, a pet ostrich and much more

Hoo Farm Animal Kingdom (Preston-on-the-Weald) Many of the animals at this jolly place seem to be treated like family pets – and in fact a pig, two foxes and an ostrich really are family pets. Notably friendly and welcoming, it's had a lot of effort put into making sure young children enjoy themselves, so though you'll find many of the expected farm activities and animals, there are a few more unusual features as well. Most obvious of these is the sheep racing, every summer afternoon (exc Fri) at 3pm; they have a Tiny Tote to place your bets. The sheep seem to enjoy their little sprint: even those not taking part that day have been known to try to join in when they hear the Tannoys. Several of the activities are under cover, notably a couple of play barns where children can bottle feed the lambs, hunt for eggs, or trundle round on a little miniature tractor circuit. Expert drivers can graduate to a new area outside. Also inside are several touch boxes and a sand pit, as well as a display of creeply-crawlies and rodents. Other features include milking demonstrations, a nature trail, a few llamas, pheasants, and a big walk-in beehive, where a glass window lets you watch the bees at work. While perhaps much of the focus is on smaller children, older ones aren't left out: for an extra charge there's quad biking for children over 6, and an air rifle range. The farm also has a Christmas tree plantation, so there's a Christmas tree maze, with a trail for toddlers to follow as they go round; busy old Father Christmas is here in December, when there are quite a few seasonal displays and activities. With so much under cover it's not a disaster if it rains, but like most farms, you'll get most out of it on a dry day. Snacks, picnic areas, shop, disabled access; cl Christmas–Mar, and maybe some autumn Mondays; (01952) 677917; £3.95 adults, £2.95 children over 2. Tickets sometimes include a free return visit. The family ticket offers a saving only if you bring three children; it's £14. Entry to the site is free in the run- up to Christmas, though there's a charge for the special displays.

57. Farm life, steam engines and ancient bicycles

Park Hall (Park Hall, Burma Rd, Oswestry) Looks at past, present and future farming techniques in restored Victorian farm buildings, with vintage farm machinery inc a working gas engine, and a collection of rare cars and bikes. Animals range from shire horses, and rare breeds of cattle, pigs, sheep and poultry, to more cuddly creatures in the pets' corner; also woodland area with unusual tree carvings and adventure playground, children's driving school (chances to test drive electric vehicles), new quad bikes, and a maze cut out of maize (summer only). With milking demon- strations (by hand or machine 1pm), and special events such as horse- and tractor-drawn carriage rides, it promises a good half- day's fun for families with smaller children; most of it is under cover. Meals, snacks, shop, good disabled access; cl 25 Dec to Feb half-term; (01691) 671123; £4.50.

Cambrian Railway Museum (Oswald Rd) Joint museum with Oswestry Cycle Museum, so lots of old bicycles and a history of cycling (esp good on Dunlop), as well as steam engines and railway memorabilia; one locomotive may be in steam bank hols and last Sun of month. They are negotiating to buy a nine-mile branch of the line nearby, so their displays may change. Snacks, shop, some disabled access; cl 25 Dec; (01691) 671749; £1.

In the bustling town itself, the Butchers Arms (Willow St) has good value food, and out at Candy to the W the Old Mill does inventive meals.

58. An interesting mix around Wrexham

Erddig (well signed S of Wrexham) Superb late 17th-c house, especially interesting for the way you can explore the life of those 'upstairs' and 'downstairs' equally as thoroughly; the gallery of servants' portraits is very touching. Enlarged and improved in the early 18th c, the house is filled with splendid original furnishings, inc a magnificent state bed in Chinese silk, and butler's pantry with silver collection. Restored outbuildings include a laundry, bake-house, estate smithy and sawmill, and the surrounding parkland is very pleasant to stroll through. It's one of the most attractive places to visit in all of Wales. Meals, snacks, shop, some disabled access; cl Thurs, Fri (open Good Fri), and Nov–Mar, house also cl am; (01978) 355314; £6, garden and outbuildings £3; NT.

The Cross Foxes at Overton Bridge, a few miles S, has good food.

Farm World (adjacent to Erddig) Well liked by readers, a 300-acre working dairy farm with all the necessary ingredients. Cl Nov–Feb; (01978) 840697; *£4.95.

Bersham Heritage Centre & Ironworks (B5099/B5098 W of Wrexham) Well re-created 18th-c ironworks, with a good overview of other local industries, and occasional demonstrations of various traditional skills. Snacks, shop, limited disabled access; Heritage Centre open all year (exc 25–26 Dec, 1 Jan); Ironworks cl Sept–Easter, best to phone for opening hours (01978) 261529; free.

59. A castle with lots for children

Bodelwyddan Castle (off A55) The walled gardens surrounding this showy white limestone castle include a glorious mix of woodland walks, flowering plants, aviary and water features. The house (older than its 19th-c exterior suggests) has been very well restored as a Victorian mansion, with furniture from the Victoria & Albert Museum, and paintings and photographs from the National Portrait Gallery. Plenty for children, inc a woodland adventure playground, and entertaining exhibitions of puzzles, games and optical illusions which they plan to extend during 2002. Snacks, shop, disabled access; cl Fri (exc July and Aug), plus Mon Nov–Mar, 25–26 Dec, 1 Jan; (01745) 584060; £4, grounds only £1.50. While you're here, have a look at the 19th-c Marble Church, built entirely of locally quarried stone: an unusual and quite splendid sight.

The Kinmel Arms at St George has good interesting food.

60. Mighty castle, tiny house

Conwy Castle One of the best-known in Wales, and one of the most important examples of military architecture in the whole of Europe. Built for Edward I in 1283–9, it's very well preserved, still looking exactly as a medieval fortress should – despite the ravages of the Civil War and beyond. There's an exhibition on Edward and the other castles he built. The tops of the turrets offer fine panoramic views; the most dramatic views of the castle itself are from the other side of the estuary. Shop; cl 24–26 Dec, 1 Jan; (01492) 592358; £3.60; Cadw.

The castle dominates the cheerful old town and was the key part of its elaborate defensive system – 21 (originally 22) towers linked by walls some 9 metres (30 ft) high, still the most complete town wall in Wales, with craggy old town gates. You can walk along some parts, looking down over the narrow little streets that still follow their medieval layout. There's a little aquarium by the quay, and you can usually go on summer boat trips. The Castle Hotel is a civilised place for lunch.

Nicely placed on the quayside is Britain's **Smallest House**, barely 2 metres (6 ft) wide and its front wall only 3 metres (10 ft) high. Squeezed into the two rooms (one up, one down) are all the comforts of home, or at least most – there's no lavatory. Shop, limited disabled access; cl Nov–Mar, Good Fri; (01492) 593484; 50p.

Butterfly Jungle (Bodlondeb Park) Tropical butterflies and exotic plants and birds in a re-created jungle environment with rain forest surround-sound; picnic area. Shop, snacks, disabled access; cl Nov–Mar; (01492) 593149; *£3.50.

Teapot World (Castle St) Splendidly silly collection of unusually shaped teapots from the last 300 years – everything from wigwams to cauliflowers. Shop; cl Oct–Mar; (01492) 593429; £1.50.

Conwy Mountain, just W of the town, has pleasant walking; not a real mountain but with views of Anglesey worthy of mountain status.

61. Family outing on Anglesey

Henblas Park (NE of Bodorgan) Good range of family activities, from sheep-shearing, falconry and farm animals, through magic shows and juggling workshops, to tractor rides and a neolithic burial chamber. Meals, snacks, shop, disabled access; cl Sat (exc bank hols), cl Oct–Feb; (01407) 840440; *£4.

You could fill a fine day along the coast of this part of the island. There are some lovely unspoilt coves and beaches around Aberffraw; the beach up the road at Rhosneigr is particularly good (and clean). And it's worth looking out for Barclodiad y Gawres. 5,000 years old, this 6-metre (20 ft) underground passage tomb at the top of the cliff is notable for the patterns carved by the entrance and in the side chambers, shown up by a good torch; it's sealed, but you can ask for a key at the Countryside Centre in Aberffraw (01407) 840845. Hard to believe now, but Aberffraw was once the capital of the north Wales kingdom of Gwynedd.

62. Anglesey sea life and farm life

Anglesey Sea Zoo (A4080 just S of Brynsiencyn) Excellent collection of local marine life, in tanks specially designed to provide as unrestricted and natural an environment as possible. Also walk-through shipwreck, touch pools, adventure playground; they sell home-made fudge and ice cream, and their own high quality sea salt. Meals, snacks, shop, disabled access; cl 18–27 Dec; (01248) 430411; £5.50.

    Foel Farm Park (Brynsiencyn) Friendly working farm with daily calf feeding, tractor rides, and home-made ice cream and chocolate. Snacks, shop, disabled access; cl late Oct–Mar; (01248) 430646; £4.25.

63. Underground slate city

Llechwedd Slate Caverns (A470, Blaenau Ffestiniog) The same company has been mining and quarrying slate here for over 150 years, and their well organised tours of the huge caverns bring the history of the site vividly to life; it's well worth doing both the underground rides. In Deep Mine, Britain's steepest passenger railway takes you 137 metres (450 ft) below the summit of the mountain. Next is a hard-hat walk through ten stunning subter-ranean chambers, each with a sound and light show illustrating the world of a Victorian miner. You need to be relatively agile (there are 61 steps going down, 71 on the way up – or did we lose count?), and bring warm clothing even in summer. The highlight is an eerie underground lake, nicely lit to create atmospheric shadows on the water and the steep, craggy walls. The other tour (the Miners Tramway) explains more about the mining process:

battery-powered trains take you around the Victorian workings, through splendid man-made caverns, some of which have tableaux or demonstrations of ancient mining skills. You get off at various points along the way, and the guides give useful talks. Outside you can explore the old buildings of Llechwedd village; the last residents left in the 1970s, but the shops and pub remain open, several stocking Victorian-themed goods which you can buy using period money; you can exchange your coins at the former bank, now a museum. Meals, snacks, shops, some disabled access with prior warning; cl 25–26 Dec, 1 Jan; (01766) 830306; both tours costs £11, just one is £7.25. The surface attractions are free.

The straggling village of Blaenau Ffestiniog is dwarfed by the vast spoil slopes from the slate mines all around it – once the slate capital of Wales, now with the passing of the industry like a living museum.

Ffestiniog Pumped Storage Power Station (Tanygrisiau, off A496 S of Blaenau Ffestiniog) Guided tours of the first hydro-electric pumped storage scheme in the country, with dramatic views towards the peaks of Snowdonia. Meals, snacks, shop; cl Sat, and end Oct–Easter; (01766) 830310; *£2.75. From the information centre there's an attractive (if slightly hairy) drive into the mountains to Stwlan Dam, which also gives super views.

At Maetwrog, further down the A496, the Grapes is a popular place for family lunches.

64. Snowdon

The best or at least the easiest way up the highest mountain in Wales is the **Snowdon Mountain Railway** (A4086, Llanberis). Britain's only public rack-and-pinion railway, with vintage Swiss steam and modern diesel locomotives. It follows the route of an old pony track, and on a good day takes passengers up over 915 metres (3,000 ft) right to the summit – where in clear weather glorious views might include the Isle of Man and the Wicklow Mountains in Ireland. It's without a doubt one of the most spectacular train journeys in the country. Trains leave when there are more than a couple of dozen people on board – so if there aren't many people about you may have to wait for it to start, and if there are you may have to queue. When trains are running to the summit, you can visit the highest postbox in England and Wales. The mountain summit is crowned by a less-than-elegant café; certainly one of the less successful works of Portmeirion architect Sir Clough Williams-Ellis, so perhaps a worthy candidate for Lottery-funded replacement. It can be chilly, so wrap up well. Meals, snacks, shop, disabled access (with notice); there's a themed gift shop down in Llanberis, and an adjacent small exhibition area; cl Nov to mid-Mar, and summit section not open till mid/late May because of weather – best to ring first; (0870) 4580033; £16.90 return.

Llanberis has plenty of B&Bs, small hotels, shops and cafés, and there are quite a few craft shops dotted along the High St. Sherpa Buses run a good service up the mountain (you can get it from several of the North Wales resorts). Just N of town is a modern working pottery; cl 2 weeks at Christmas; (01286) 676120; free.

This whole area has plenty of fine walking, both gentle and taxing. The main mountain group soars dramatically, and many of its peaks have easily identifiable shapes (when you can see them through the mist). Snowdon itself, the highest mountain in England or Wales, has a number of paths up ranging from the easy one alongside the mountain railway to the enthralling Horseshoe Route, which makes its way along knife-edge ridges; the Pyg Track and Watkin Path are among the favourites. For a taste of the mountain without actually going up it, follow the start of the Miners' Track (from the Pen-y-pass car park on the A4086), which really is a track as far as Glaslyn, the last of four lakes passed. The National Trust now owns large areas of the mountain, and is carrying out path improvements alongside careful conservation of the landscape – perhaps with eventual regeneration of some former oak forest.

65. From Celts and King Arthur to an eco-friendly 21st century

Celtica (Machynlleth) Very enjoyable look at the history and legends of the Celts, in an 18th-c mansion. There's a traditionalish museum upstairs, but more fun is the lively walk-through exhibition on the ground floor, special effects bringing ancient villages and druids' prophecies vividly to life. Also a good themed indoor play area for under-8s. It's popular with school trips the last couple of weeks of term. Meals, snacks, good shop, disabled access; cl 24–26 Dec, 1 Jan; (01654) 702702; £4.95.

Centre for Alternative Technology (A487 3m N) Technologies for the improvement of the environment have been researched and displayed at this enthusiastic place for over 20 years now, with constantly updated demonstrations of wind power, wave power and solar energy – you can even ride a water-powered cliff railway (one of Britain's steepest; Easter–Oct only). A fun exhibition shows what it's like to be in a mole hole. The site, an old slate quarry, has fine Snowdonia views, and they look after children well. Wholesome vegetarian restaurant, good bookshop, disabled access; cl Christmas and 2 wks in Jan; (01654) 705950/702400; £7. They do good value family tickets, and you can save 10% if you arrive by bus, bike or foot; you can also halve the cost of hiring a bike from Greenstiles in Machynlleth, (01654) 703543.

King Arthur's Labyrinth (Upper Corris, off A487 towards Corris Uchaf) Fun for families; a boat trip takes you to the heart of the underground tunnels and caverns, then it's a half-mile walk through passageways punctuated with scenes from the local version of the Arthurian legends. Wrap up well: it can get cold down here. Meals, snacks, shop; cl mid-Nov to end Mar; (01654) 761584; £4.55.

The Dyfi Valley Pass costing £13.50 covers all three attractions. In Machynlleth, the White Lion, a big country-town bar, does decent lunches inc vegetarian.

Scotland

SEE MAP 4

◆ ◆ ◆

1. Culzean Castle

(pronounced 'Cullane') A day here is one of the most popular outings in the region. The 18th-c mansion is one of great presence and brilliance, and the 563 acres of grounds are among the finest in Britain, lushly planted and richly ornamental, with woods, lake, an abundance of paths, bracing clifftop and shoreline walks, and an 18th-c walled garden. The house was splendidly refashioned by Robert Adam, and has been well restored to show off his work to full effect. Meals, snacks, shop, disabled access; house open Apr-Oct, and possibly some winter wknds, park open all year; (01655) 884455; £8 park and castle, £3.50 park only; NTS. You can stay in rather smart self-contained apartments on the top floor.

2. Boat trip to Arran

Subtropical gardens, archaeological sites and mountain deer forest make this a wonderfully rewarding island. Arran is as famous for the diversity of its geology and for its beautifully set and highly regarded golf courses as for its coastal and mountain walking. It is just under an hour by ferry from Ardrossan, a popular public-transport day trip from Glasgow, with summer ferries from Claonaig on Kintyre too; (01475) 650100 for ferry enquiries. Brodick the main settlement has several places to hire bikes. The Kingsley on Brodick esplanade has decent home cooking, and the

Ormidale Hotel has good value food. On the opposite side of the island nr Machrie are several intriguing Bronze Age stone circles. Arran has a good circular walk up and down Goatfell, prominent for miles around, and you can follow the shore right around the N tip, the Cock of Arran. Up nr here the waterside Catacol Hotel has decent food. There's a good walk on the W coast, from Blackwaterfoot to the King's Cave, which supposedly sheltered Robert the Bruce.

Brodick Castle The island's jewel, this fine old castle is in lovely surroundings between the sea, hills and majestic mountain of Goatfell. Partly 13th-c, and extended in 1652 and 1844, it's very fierce-looking from the outside, but comfortably grand inside – even a little homely in places. There are almost a hundred antlered heads on the walls of the main staircase. It's surrounded by magnificent formal gardens, with the highlight the woodland garden started in 1923 by the Duchess of Montrose, inc many lovely rare and tender rhododendrons. Meals, snacks, shop, limited disabled access; castle cl Nov–Mar, garden and country park open all year; (01770) 302202; £6; NTS.

3. Scotland's heroes and thundering waterfalls

Discover Carmichael Visitor Centre (Carmichael; A73 N of Biggar) Among the eclectic attractions here are a collection of waxwork models of Scotland's heroes and heroines, various period re-creations inc a Victorian wash-house, a baby animal farm, free horse and cart rides, and an exhibition on wind energy, all within the attractive grounds of the Carmichael Estate. Also outdoor adventure play areas, buggy racing and a deer park walk; meals, snacks, farm shop specialising in home reared meat, disabled access; cl Jan–Mar, Apr and May open by appointment; (01899) 308169; £3.25.

Falls of Clyde (New Lanark) The countryside here is

spectacular, with a short walk snaking around river cliffs through a verdant gorge to these falls that used to power the mill; a visitor centre here has lots of information on badgers (cl before 11am, and 25–26 Dec). The falls are dramatic when the hydro-electric station upriver opens the sluices.

New Lanark (off A73) Founded in 1785 and now the subject of a major conservation programme, this is Scotland's best example of an industrial village, with plenty to keep families amused for a good chunk of the day. Many of the old millworkers' buildings (showing living conditions of the 1820s and 1930s) have been interestingly converted to modern accommodation, so it's very much a living village rather than a museum. The recently refurbished village store has an exhibition about Robert Owen's original store, and his house contains an exhibition on his work. The village can be busy at wknds; try to visit during the week if you can. There's a new time travel ride at the visitor centre. Meals, snacks, shop, disabled access; cl before 11am, 25 Dec, 1 Jan; *£4.75.

In Lanark itself the Crown (Hope St) has a decent restaurant.

4. Queen of the Clyde

Clydebuilt (Braehead Shopping Centre, off junctions 25a and 26 of M8) The Glaswegian extension of the Scottish Maritime Museum in Irvine tells the story of Glasgow and the Clyde from the tobacco lords of the 17th c, through the city's important status as a global centre for shipbuilding, right up to the present day. Interactive exhibits let you steer your own ship or make a fortune as an ocean trader, and for a taste of the real thing you can take control of a real steam engine and go aboard the oldest Clyde-built vessel still afloat. Shop, disabled access; cl 25 Dec and 1 Jan; (0141) 886 1013; £3.50.

Museum of Transport (Kelvin Hall, Bunhouse Rd, Glasgow)

Comprehensive collection of vehicles, from trams to ships, very well displayed; the walk-through car showroom is arranged as if some were for sale, with original prices displayed on the windscreens. Snacks, shop, disabled access; cl 25–26 Dec, 1–2 Jan; (0141) 287 2720; free.

Linn Park (Cathcart/Castlemilk) Lots to do – riverside walks, nature trails, golf course, as well as a ruined 14th-c castle, an adventure playground for the disabled (prior arrangement preferred), and an equestrian centre; (0141) 637 3096. Visitor centre open most wknd pms; (0141) 637 1147; free.

5. Glasgow Science Centre

(Pacific Quay) An amazing new draw on the banks of the Clyde, opposite the Scottish Exhibition Centre, this is Britain's biggest and perhaps most exciting science centre and by far the largest Millennium project north of the border. There are three main attractions: the four-storey Science Mall, the remarkable 100-metre (328-ft) Glasgow Tower, and the IMAX theatre. All are extraordinary-looking: the Mall and the theatre are the only buildings in Europe apart from Bilbao's Guggenheim to be clad in shimmering titanium, while the tower is the only one in the world capable of revolving 360 degrees from the ground up. Exploring them all will easily fill a varied and interesting whole day, and the Science Mall on its own can take four hours. The most appealing part for families, this has hundreds of interactive and hands-on displays, a planetarium, and an ambitious virtual reality theatre, with unique journeys through space stations and the human body shown on a massive screen that fills all your peripheral vision. One floor concentrates on fairly basic science, with plenty of simple experiments and activities for children (and a soft play area for younger ones). Particularly good fun is the optical illusion section –

if you stare at one spinning disc of light for long enough, then turn to look at someone, you'll be amazed at what happens to the shape of their face. The next floor up has slightly more complex activities showing science in action, all with touch-screen instructions; there's an especially enjoyable section where you can build your own vehicle and race it round a track running the length of the building. Another floor has touch-screen displays on how science affects our lives, in health, medicine, and the environment; exhibitions cover advances from Laika the Space Dog to Dolly the Sheep. Dotted around all over the place are what they call Discovery areas – small spaces where you can crack on with your own experiments. Meanwhile the Tower has more traditional displays and presentations on past and future developments in Glasgow, as well as splendid views from the top. The IMAX theatre (Scotland's first) shows off huge films currently ranging from an underwater swim with dolphins, a trip through Egypt and an all too realistic thrill ride. It's all indoors, so good in any weather, and though seeing it all costs a bit more than many of the city's attractions, it's excellent value considering the range and quality of what's here. Meals, snacks, shop, disabled access; cl 25 Dec, 1 Jan; (0141) 420 5000. You can buy individual tickets for each attraction: £6.50 (£4.50 children) for the Science Mall, and £5.50 (£4 children) for the Tower or the IMAX; but it's better value to get a double ticket if you want to do two of them (£9.50 adults, £7 children) or a triple ticket if you've time to do everything (£14 adults, £10 children). There's a sensible variety of family tickets, rather than just assuming as most places do that all families are the same size.

Cheerful Di Maggios (Ruthven Lane) is a famous Glasgow Italian restaurant, nice for a treat and not too dear. Children are also welcome for good value pub lunches at the Auctioneers (North Court, St Vincent Pl) and Babbity Bowster (Blackfriars St), both of them unusual and entertaining places.

6. A free day out in Glasgow

People's Palace (Glasgow Green) Very enjoyable refurbished social history museum looking at Glaswegians over the centuries, in a park just SE of centre; disabled access; cl 25 Dec, 1–2 Jan; (0141) 5540 223; free. The museum's café is in the adjacent Winter Gardens, a massive conservatory with huge tropical plants.

    Scotland Street School Museum Designed by Mackintosh, this spectacular building originally had a capacity of 1,250 pupils in 21 classrooms, and now houses a lively museum with fun recreations and interesting exhibits dedicated to education. Cl 25–26 Dec, 1–2 Jan (0141) 287 0500; free.

    Pollok Country Park (SW of centre) One of the best of the several parks and gardens you'll find around Glasgow, with waterside and woodland trails, rose garden, Clydesdale horses and highland cattle. Shop, snacks, disabled access; (0141) 632 9299; free.

7. Edinburgh's Royal Mile

The evocative heart of Edinburgh's Old Town, this runs down from the Castle to the Palace of Holyrood, which stands on the edge of the fine open spaces around the mini-mountain of Arthur's Seat. Besides the must-see places we describe (in order, heading down from the Castle), thoroughly recommendable but more grown-up places along the Mile are the Scotch Whisky Heritage Centre (Castlehill, £6.50), Gladstone's Land (fine early 17th-c building, Lawnmarket, £3.50), Lady Stair's House (another 17th-c building with a Scottish writers' museum, off Lawnmarket, free), St Giles Cathedral (free), Parliament House (the seat of Scottish government until 1707 and now Scotland's supreme court, Parliament Sq, free), John Knox House (the oldest house on the Mile, High St, £2.25 –

may cl from Sept 2002 for refurbishment), and the Museum of Edinburgh (fine collections, even Greyfriars Bobby's collar and bowl, Canongate, free). There are plenty of refreshment places along the Mile, and no shortage of tourist shops.

Edinburgh Castle Perched on its hill above the city, this is a place of great magnetism; it's been a fortress since at least the 7th c, and excavations show there's been a settlement here for 4,000 years. The oldest building today is the beautiful St Margaret's Chapel, thought to have been built in the 12th c and little changed since. Other highlights include the apartments of Mary, Queen of Scots, Mons Meg (the 15th-c Belgian cannon with which James II cowed the Black Douglases), the Scottish Crown Jewels (centuries older than the English ones), and for romantics the Stone of Destiny or Scottish coronation stone; the polished natural rock protruding into the building also stays in the memory. Glorious views from the battlements, over the Firth of Forth to Fife beyond. You can wander around on your own, but the official guides are a great bonus – they leave from the drawbridge, several times a day. Meals, snacks, shop, mostly disabled access; cl 25–26 Dec; (0131) 225 9846; £7.50 (inc audio tour); HS. If you're around at lunchtime, look (and listen) for the firing of the One o' Clock Gun from the parapet.

Camera Obscura (Castlehill) These 19th-c revolving lenses and mirrors create unique panoramas of the city as soon as the lights go down, with a good commentary; best on a sunny day. Shop; cl 25 Dec; (0131) 226 3709; £4.50.

Museum of Childhood (High St) The first of its type and still one of the best, a charming collection of games, toys and dolls from all over the globe. Shop, some disabled access; cl Sun (exc pm during Festival and July–Aug); (0131) 529 4142; free.

Canongate Tolbooth (Canongate) This elaborate building houses an excellent social history exhibition, the People's Story, with reconstructions built very much around first-hand accounts of Edinburgh life. Shop, disabled access; cl Sun (exc pm during Festival), 25–26 Dec, 1 Jan; (0131) 529 4057; free.

Dynamic Earth (Holyrood Rd) This exemplary exhibition shows the story of the planet using hi-tech effects and state-of-the-art displays. It vividly relates the story of evolution using giant screens, dramatic sounds and commentary, and evocative smells, spread over eleven hugely different and often quite spectacular display areas. You can see a volcano erupt, experience an earthquake, watch animals swinging through trees in the rain forest, and take a helicopter flight over the glaciers of Scandinavia. The finale is a colourful film taking in images of storms, hurricanes, and sunsets, with a serious environmental message of course – but hearing it has rarely been so much fun; play area for younger children. Meals, snacks, shop, disabled access; cl Mon and Tues between Nov and Mar, and 24–25 Dec; (0131) 550 7800; £7.95.

Palace of Holyroodhouse (Canongate) Imposing yet human-scale palace with its origins in the Abbey of Holyrood, founded by David I. Later the court of Mary, Queen of Scots, it was used by Bonnie Prince Charlie during his occupation of Edinburgh, and is still a Royal residence for part of the year. The oldest surviving part is James IV's tower, with Queen Mary's rooms on the second floor, where a plaque on the floor marks where her secretary Rizzio was murdered in front of her. The throne room and state rooms have period furniture, tapestries and paintings from the Royal Collection. Much more inviting than many English palaces, and in the last few years they've really improved visitor facilities. In summer there's a path through the palace gardens, which will be recovering from all the works linked to construction of the new space-age home for the Scottish Parliament opposite, its original £50 million budget already in tatters as costs soar to £250 million. Shop, limited disabled access by prior arrangement; cl Good Fri,

25–26 Dec, and occasional other dates (if the Queen is in residence for example) – best to check first on (0131) 556 7371; £6.50.

8. Edinburgh Zoo

(Corstorphine Rd; A8 W) Best known for its Penguin Parade most afternoons at 2.15 (Apr–Oct); there are plenty of other rare and odd-looking animals around the attractive grounds. Children enjoy the yew-hedge maze loosely themed around Darwin's theory of evolution; it has several fountains along the way that periodically shoot out jets of water (summer only). Extra events and activities in summer hols. Meals, snacks, shops, disabled access (though a little hilly); open every day (inc 25 Dec); (0131) 334 9171; £7.

9. The sky's the limit

Royal Observatory (Blackford Hill, Edinburgh) An interactive science centre with hands-on exhibits about light, CD-Roms about space and astronomy, and Scotland's largest telescope showing a panoramic view of Edinburgh; info about the past and present work of the observatory; temporary exhibitions, special events, astronomy classes, and evening tours. Snacks, shop, limited disabled access; cl 24 Dec–3 Jan; (0131) 668 8405; £3.50.

Royal Museum/Museum of Scotland (Chambers St, Edinburgh) A tremendous variety of collections, covering virtually anything you might care to poke around in, now shared between a gloriously light and spacious Victorian building, and its grand new counterpart next door. Children particularly enjoy the intricate working scale models of early engines, but it has something for everyone. Meals, snacks, shop, disabled access; cl Sun am and 25 Dec; (0131) 225 7534; free.

10. A busy day out in Stirling

Too much really to squeeze into one day – but you'll really enjoy this historic yet thoroughly unstuffy small town, and can pick and choose to suit you.

Stirling Castle Provides magnificent views from its lofty hilltop site. It became very popular with the Royal Family in the 15th and 16th c, and most of the buildings date from that period. The finest features are the Chapel Royal built by James VI (and I of England), and the Renaissance palace built by James V. A 10-year restoration project has transformed the Great Hall back to its early 16th-c grandeur; crowning the work is a huge new hammerbeam roof made from 350 oak trees and erected by the same craftsmen who assembled the new roof in St George's Hall, Windsor Castle, after the fire of 1992. Snacks, shop; cl 25–26 Dec; (01786) 450000; £6.50 (the ticket includes entry to Argyll's Lodging), parking £2; HS. There's a good visitor centre in a restored building next door.

Whistlebinkies (St Mary's Wynd), formerly part of the ancient castle stables but wholly modernised inside, has decent food.

Argyll's Lodging Built by Sir William Alexander, founder of Nova Scotia, and then passed on to the Earls of Argyll, this is the finest surviving example of a 17th-c town house in Scotland. Used as an army barracks and hospital, and then a Youth Hostel, the main rooms have now been re-created to look as they would have done in around 1680. Shop; cl 25–26 Dec, phone for opening times over New Year; (0131) 668 8800.

Wallace Monument (top of Abbey Craig, just NE) Perhaps Stirling's most satisfying attraction, a huge 67-metre (220-ft) Victorian tower with dramatic views from the top of its 246 spiralling steps. Each floor has lively audio-visual displays, one on Sir William Wallace, another examining other Scottish heroes. There is a statue of Wallace as portrayed by Mel Gibson in *Braveheart* in the car park. Snacks, shop; cl 25, 31 Dec, 1 Jan; (01786) 472140; £3.95.

Old Town Jail (St John St) In season, actor-led tours take you through the preserved cells of this 19th-c jail (there's a self-guided audio tour at other times), and there's a new exhibition on prison life today. A glass-sided lift takes you up to roof-top views over the town. Shop, disabled access; cl 25–26 Dec, 1 Jan; (01786) 450050; £3.95.

11. Safari and Adventure

(A84, Blair Drummond) Wild animals in natural surroundings, with plenty of other activities included in the price, from gentle rides for younger children to the exhilarating Flying Fox slide over the lake. You can explore part of the water in pedal-boats, and boat trips circle Chimpanzee Island leaving the chimps to enjoy their natural habitat undisturbed; one of the chimps made the news recently by stealing a keeper's mobile phone and making anonymous calls with it. Feeding times of lions, sea lions, and penguins are posted in the park. Meals, snacks, shop, disabled access; cl Oct–Mar; (01786) 841456; £8.50 (£4.50 children 3–14) – not bad value if you bring a barbie and make a half-day of it.

The Lion & Unicorn on the A873 at Thornhill does good family lunches. To fill out a longer day you could link that with a drive via Aberfoyle (lots of woollens shops and lovely forest scenery) and the A821 through the Trossachs (the Highlands in miniature, beautiful lochs and glens) to Callander (plenty more for visitors here). On the way, the Lade Inn at Kilmahog and Byre at Brig o' Turk are two more good food stops.

12. Deep-Sea World

(North Queensferry) The highlight of this fantastically elaborate aquarium is the spectacular underwater safari. Moving walkways carry you along a transparent viewing tunnel as long as a football pitch, surrounded by all kinds of underwater creatures, and a million gallons of water; it's divided into different areas to group together the various species, and you'll generally see a few divers too, hand-feeding the fish or taking part in question and answer sessions thanks to waterproof communication systems. The sea-horses are popular, and you can stroke some of the creatures kept in the rock-pools (inc a shark). A new exhibit, Deep Sea Explorer, allows you to pilot an underwater vehicle. There's a good programme of talks, activities and feeding displays, and the free behind-the-scenes tours give a good insight into the demands of looking after so many creatures, and an introduction to their successful breeding and conservation programmes. They also have a good collection of amphibians, taking in the world's most poisonous frog, and some snakes. Meals, snacks, shop, disabled access; cl 25 Dec; (01383) 411880; £6.50 (inc face-painting).

Inchcolm Abbey Much-raided medieval ruins on a memorable island site out in the Firth of Forth, reached by a ferry trip from North Queensferry (weather permitting); open Apr-Sept (exc Sun am); (0131) 331 4857; £2.80; HS. There's also a ferry from South Queensferry, on the other side of the Firth – notable for its views of the two great Forth bridges on either side, with piers to potter on; the Hawes Inn, famous from *Kidnapped*, is still going strong and a nice place for lunch.

13. A day out in Dundee

Sensation (Greenmarket) This fun science centre claims to be the only one in Europe devoted entirely to the senses. With more than 60 interactive exhibits, the emphasis is certainly on hands-on fun. Displays range from a giant head which children can climb through (they can even slide out of the nose), to a soft-play area (you can fire balls from a cannon) and various computer-based games inc one based on germination, with individual seeds clamouring for your attention – you have to choose what they need to make them grow. Snacks, shop, disabled access; cl 25–26 Dec, 1 Jan; (01382) 228800; £5 (£3.50 children).

Camperdown Country Park (off A90) 400 acres of fine parkland with golf course, nature trails, woodland footpaths, and wildlife centre with indigenous animals from wolves and bears to wildcats. Also adventure play area themed around the defeat of the Dutch at the 1797 Battle of Camperdown. Snacks, shop, disabled access; cl Christmas and New Year; (01382) 432689; free, £2.10 wildlife centre.

In Dundee, the Chequers (South Tay St), Royal Oak (Brook St – Indian), Mercantile (Commercial St) and Number 1 (Constitution Rd) all do good value food.

14. Highland wildlife and traditions

Highland Wildlife Park (B9152, Kincraig) Owned by the same charity as Edinburgh Zoo, this 260-acre wildlife park somehow manages to seem a bit wilder than most animal attractions; perhaps it's because they specialise in species once native to the area, so you really get a feeling that the animals could have wandered out of the surrounding woods and mountains. You drive safari-style around enclosures of reindeer, wildcats and enormous bison. The most exciting feature is the wolf territory, where a walkway takes you to a safe vantage point right in the heart of the enclosure. Plenty of rare breeds, inc the wild Przewalksi's horses, one of the world's rarest mammals, and you may see red squirrels feeding in the forest; daily talks and wknd summer face-painting. Snacks and shop in visitor centre, disabled access; cl Nov–Mar in bad weather, so best to check; (01540) 651270; £6.50.

In Kingussie (pronounced Kinoossie) the Royal is useful for lunch (and now brews its own beer). For the next part of this day out, choose between these next two – the Folk Park is on a much bigger scale, so is much more expensive:

Highland Folk Museum (Duke St, Kingussie) The first open-air museum with reconstructed buildings in Britain, originally opened on Iona in 1935. Exhibits provide an insight into the social history of the ordinary people of the Highlands inc a reconstructed Isle of Lewis black house. Shop, disabled access; cl Sun, wknds Oct–Mar, Christmas and New Year (open for guided tours only in winter); (01540) 661307; £1.

Highland Folk Park (A86 E of Kingussie) On 85 acres, this reconstructed 18th-c settlement is the Folk Museum's younger but bigger out-of-town offshoot: you can see a Victorian water-powered sawmill, curling hut, pre-war school (with many original fittings) and clock-maker's workshop. Costumed guides help bring history to life, and vintage buses transport you round the site. Snacks, shop, audio-visual centre, disabled access, play area. Open daily Apr–Aug, wkdys Sept–Oct; (01540) 673551; £5.

15. Forest discoveries

Landmark Heritage & Adventure Park (Carrbridge) Good family day out, with exhibition on the microscopic world, well signposted forest trails (one through the tree-tops), a new covered, elaborate adventure playground (children 5–14), water-coaster, and Forestry Heritage Park with fully operational steam-powered sawmill (Apr–Oct). You can sometimes have a go at log-cutting and Flex the giant Clydesdale horse may be hauling logs to the mill. Great views from the top of the viewing tower. Meals, snacks, shop, disabled access; cl 25 Dec; (01479) 841614; £6.95.

The Dalrachney Lodge Hotel does good lunches.

16. A day out around Inveraray

Argyll Wildlife Park (Dalchenna; A83 SW) A collection of local or once-local animals (deer, foxes and wildcats) plus chipmunks, wallabies, racoons and so forth – with some eminently tame wild creatures wandering around. Snacks, shop, disabled access; cl Nov–Easter; (01499) 302264; £4.

Inveraray Jail (Church Sq) Excellent prison museum, with costumed guides and Katie the Governor's cow really bringing the place to life. You can watch a trial, try your hand at hard labour, and even experience being locked up in one of the sparse little cells. Watch out for the animated surprises. Shop; cl 25 Dec, 1 Jan; (01499) 302381; £4.95.

In beautifully placed waterside Inveraray, the Loch Fyne Hotel is pleasant for lunch, with stunning views; the George is popular too.

17. Scotland's wildest places

Torridon Countryside Centre (junction A896 and Diabaig rd) Gateway to a huge area of nature reserve in stunning mountain scenery – some say the best in Scotland. It has displays on the scenery and wildlife, as well as a deer park and deer museum. Visitor centre cl Sun am, and all Oct–Apr; £1.50; (01445) 791221; NTS. Nearby at the Mains there are herds of red deer and Highland cattle. Torridon is wonderful for challenging walks, and there are a few outstanding easier ones, based for example on Loch Torridon's shores. The Kinlochewe Hotel (A896 E) has decent food; to reach anywhere N of here by car from the S, incidentally, it's much quicker to go by Inverness than to make your way all the way up the W coast.

MAPS

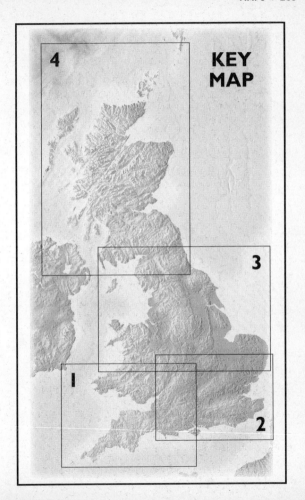

4

KEY
MAP

3

1

2

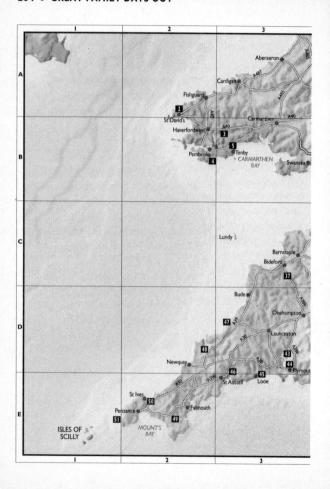

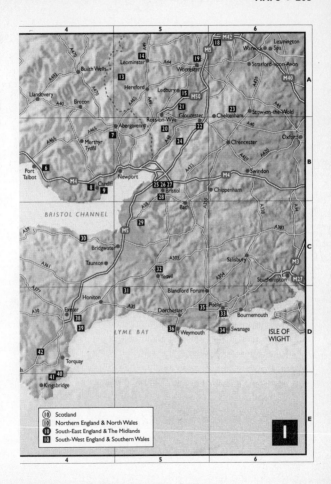

(10) Scotland
(10) Northern England & North Wales
(10) South-East England & The Midlands
(10) South-West England & Southern Wales

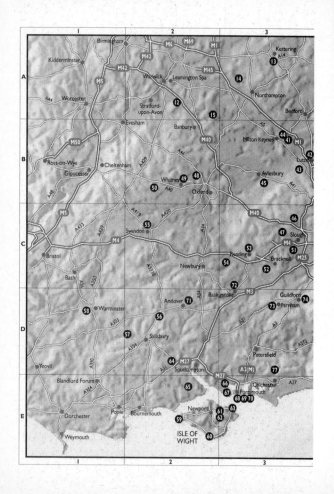

Scotland

Northern England & North Wales

South-East England & The Midlands

South-West England & Southern Wales

2

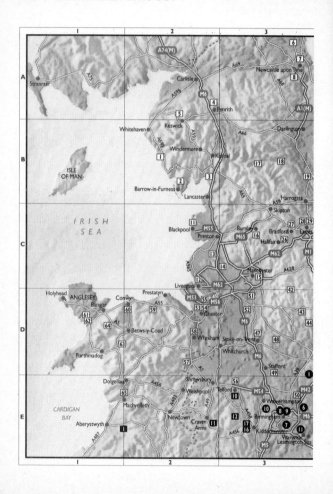

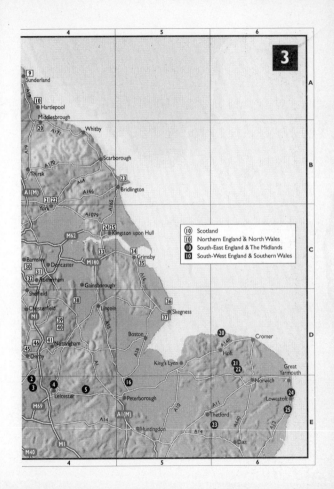

3

Legend:
- 10 Scotland
- 10 Northern England & North Wales
- 10 South-East England & The Midlands
- 10 South-West England & Southern Wales

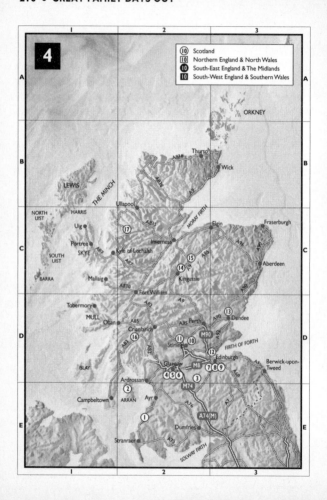

All Ebury titles are available in good bookshops or via mail order

TO ORDER
(please tick)

Pocket Good Guide to Great Food Pubs	£5.99
The Good Pub Guide	£14.99
The Good Britain Guide	£14.99
The Good Hotel Guide to UK and Ireland	£15.99
The Good Hotel Guide to Continental Europe	£16.99

PAYMENT MAY BE MADE USING ACCESS, VISA, MASTERCARD, DINERS CLUB, SWITCH AND AMEX OR CHEQUE, EUROCHEQUE AND POSTAL ORDER (STERLING ONLY)

CARD NUMBER:

EXPIRY DATE:............   SWITCH ISSUE NO:.................

SIGNATURE:...

PLASE ALLOW £2.50 FOR POST AND PACKAGING FOR THE FIRST BOOK AND £1.00 THEREAFTER

ORDER TOTAL: £   (INC P&P)

ALL ORDERS TO:

EBURY PRESS, BOOKS BY POST, TBS LIMITED, COLCHESTER ROAD, FRATING GREEN, COLCHESTER, ESSEX CO7 7DW, UK

TELEHONE:	01206 256 000
FAX:	01206 255 914

NAME:

ADDRESS:

Please allow 28 days for delivery. Please tick box if you do not wish to receive any additional information

Prices and availability subject to change without notice.